TRAPPIST BEER TRAVELS

INSIDE THE BREWERIES OF THE MONASTERIES

Schiffer Publishing Ltd

4880 Lower Valley Road • Atglen, PA 19310

BY CAROLINE WALLACE, SARAH WOOD, AND JESSICA DEAHL

Library of Congress Control Number: 2017932267

Cover design by Jessica Deahl,
cover layout by John Cheek
Type set in Bebas Neue/Bell MT

ISBN: 978-0-7643-5294-2
Printed in China

Published by Schiffer Publishing, Ltd.
4880 Lower Valley Road
Atglen, PA 19310
Phone: (610) 593-1777; Fax: (610) 593-2002
E-mail: Info@schifferbooks.com
Web: www.schifferbooks.com

For our complete selection of fine books on this
and related subjects, please visit our website at
www.schifferbooks.com. You may also write
for a free catalog.

Schiffer Publishing's titles are available at special
discounts for bulk purchases for sales promotions or
premiums. Special editions, including personalized
covers, corporate imprints, and excerpts, can be
created in large quantities for special needs.
For more information, contact the publisher.

We are always looking for people to write books
on new and related subjects. If you have an
idea for a book, please contact us at
proposals@schifferbooks.com.

Contents

Acknowledgments 004

Introduction 005

01. Trappist Origins. 008

02. Orval 017

03. Achel 037

04. La Trappe 051

05. Rochefort 071

06. Chimay. 089

07. Westvleteren 107

08. Westmalle 125

09. Zundert 139

10. Stift Engelszell 153

11. Tre Fontane. 171

12. Spencer. 183

13. Contemplation. 198

References. 202

Glossary 206

Acknowledgments

Without the help of each of the following individuals, our project would not have been possible. We offer our deepest gratitude to:

Christine Boucquillon and Brother Xavier Frisque with the International Trappist Association; Philippe Henroz and the Orval Abbey Community; Benoît Minet, Brother Gregoire and the Notre-Dame de Saint-Remy Abbey Community; Fabrice Bordon, Edwin Dedoncker, Jérôme Goffinet, and the Scourmont Abbey Community; Marc Knops, Jordy Theuwen, and the Achel Abbey Community; Brother Benedikt Van Overstraeten, Philippe Van Assche, and the Westmalle Abbey Community; Elske Vugts, Danielle Leukel, Brother Isaac Majoor, and the Koningshoeven Abbey Community; Brother Godfried, Brother Joris, and the Saint-Sixtus Abbey Community; Brother Christiaan, Brother Guido, and the Maria Toevlucht Abbey Community; Jenny Jungwirth, Dom Marianus, and the Engelszell Abbey Community; Father Isaac Keeley, Mary Jeffcoat, and the Saint Joseph's Abbey Community; and Sergio and Cristiana Daniele, Father Danilo, and the Tre Fontane Abbey Community.

Also our amazing interpreters Filip "Phil" Muylle, Océane Crabbe, Linda Mous, Bart Westerveld, and Alina Brückner; Pete Schiffer and the rest of the team at Schiffer Publishing; Chuck Cook, Jen Naugler, Grady Wright, the Studium team, Nick Pugliese, and the team at Austin Beerworks; Independence Brewing Company; Austin Beer Garden Brewing Company; Pinthouse Pizza; Hops & Grain Brewery; Blue Owl Brewing; Real Ale Brewing Company; Live Oak Brewing Company; Black Star Co-Op; Rogness Brewing Company; Isaac Menge (Lady Lazarus); Jody Reyes and the team at WhichCraft Beer Shop; Tara Carr and the ladies of Pink Boots Society Central Texas; Craft Pride; our generous Blog-a-Thon donors, Eric Yohe, Ashley Rendon, Ryan Matlock, David Mitchell, Andrea Sanchez, Ari Auber, Pam Catoe, Jo Hunter, Mike Lambert, Dita Malaer, Mar Turner, Rachel Fausett, Davy Pasternak, Danielle Hinch, Suzy Shaffer, Lucas Pagan, Drew Johnson, Katie Gustainis Vela, Bryan Koroleski, Bill Doughty, Robert Garese, Daytona Camps, Rachel Hackathorn, Kyle Varga, Nathan Merrick, Beverly Martin, Russell Castillo Jr., Sara Partridge, Mike Bostick, Tre Miner, Callie Fagen, Jon Partridge, Becky Stack, Hayden Royal, Spencer Cox, Derrick Steele, Daniel Doherty, and Bret Stewart; Dan Black; Carlos Arellano; Patrick Hernandez; and the ever-supportive ladies of BitchBeer.org. Extra thanks for the tremendous support of the Deahl family, the Wallace family, and the Wood family.

Introduction

Somewhere over the Atlantic the magnitude of the adventure we were about to embark on finally hit the three of us. It had been ten months since we first dreamed up the idea for this book, a plan hatched over a few impromptu pints of beer spiked with a dose of wanderlust. If those months spent making extensive travel arrangements and corresponding over e-mail with Trappist monks did not convince us it was really happening, now watching our cartoon plane clear Newfoundland and glide over open ocean on the seatback's glowing "Live Flight Tracking" feature was starting to do the trick.

With roots tracing back to the eleventh century, the Order of Cistercians of the Strict Observance (OCSO)—more commonly referred to as Trappists—are a Roman Catholic religious order of cloistered, contemplative monks who live a devoted life balanced between prayer, study, and work in a variety of trades to financially sustain the needs of their monasteries. Some of these monasteries produce high quality handmade goods like bread, cheeses, and religious paraphernalia to fulfill this mission, but it is the small segment of Trappist monasteries in Europe and North America who have set up world-renowned breweries within their walls that captured our fascination.

For a group of American beer writers, the prospect of making a journey to every Trappist brewery is pretty much the dream of a lifetime. As notorious for being closed off from the

(From left to right) Authors Caroline Wallace, Sarah Wood, and Jessica Deahl. *Patrick Hernandez*

outside world as they are for their exceptional brews, the Trappists served as a source of wonder since our early days exploring the nuances of this beverage. While our palates were intimately familiar with the flavors of world class beers like Chimay Grande Réserve Blue and Rochefort 10, our impressions of the Trappist monks and their philosophies for living, worshiping, and brewing were formed on little more than hearsay. This dichotomy was what inspired us to leave the glow of our computer screens in Austin, Texas, to visit the beer brewing Trappist abbeys of Belgium, the Netherlands, Austria, Italy, and finally just outside of Boston, Massachusetts, in a quest to experience, taste, and learn more.

As these fingers touch the keys, monks at eleven of the world's Trappist abbeys are currently brewing beers labeled "Authentic Trappist Products." The pages to follow will tell their stories, along with what it takes to earn this distinction. When we originally dreamed up the idea for this book there were only ten of these breweries.

Our original idea was to visit all ten in a whirlwind "Amazing Race" style trip, stopping at one per day and then on to the next. In retrospect, while that plan may have lent a catchiness to the book title à la *Visiting the World's Ten Trappist Breweries in Ten Days*, it would not have been in line with the Trappist emphasis on contemplation.

Fate intervened when Tre Fontane, an abbey in Rome where monastic life goes back to the early years of Christianity, began brewing beer within the abbey walls. Tre Fontane obtained the "Authentic Trappist Product" certification from the International Trappist Association while we were in the beginning stages of planning our trip. Faced with an extra stop (and let's face it, *Eleven Trappist Breweries in Eleven Days* doesn't have quite the same ring to it), we expanded our plans and set upon a still aggressive but slightly more contemplative itinerary that included taking an overnight train to Rome to visit the newest addition. So, over the course of eighteen days in June 2015, we visited all eleven, beginning at Orval Abbey, in Belgium's Gaume region, and ending stateside just outside of Boston at Saint Joseph Abbey, which houses Spencer Brewery.

Armed with cameras, notebooks, recording devices (see: iPhone), and in most cases interpreters, we traveled from abbey to abbey, meeting with monks and the laypeople who work alongside them in their breweries. The order of the trip was partially established by geography and partially by our interview subjects' schedules. The result of these interviews, experiences, and subsequent research is now sitting in your hands, organized by the crisscrossing trajectory of the journey.

Within these pages we will explore what makes Trappist beers different from export "abbey beers" donning images of those oh-so-cheeky monks and how these breweries operate unlike any others. We will dig into the history, spirit, and beers of each individual abbey. Should you want to make a journey of your own, we will tell you where to go and what to see. It is important to note while nearly all Trappist breweries are closed to visitors, most of the abbeys have some aspects (be it a gift shop, a tasting room across the street, or an open house once per year) that are open to the public.

As interest in craft beer (or as the Belgians sometimes call them, "special beers") rises stateside and abroad, it is clear these seminal brewers have had a resounding impact on beer drinkers the world over. In America many craft beer aficionados today would perhaps never have discovered their love for the beverage had they not decided decades ago to reach for an unfamiliar export beer called Chimay at their local bar instead of one of the usual big three light lagers on tap. Known for their character, quality, and complexity, Trappist beers have inspired generations of beer drinkers with new ideas about what beer could and can be.

One last important disclaimer: As with most things in life, this book is best enjoyed with a glass of excellent beer in hand, so grab your favorite Trappist beer—or better yet one to pair with each chapter—and enjoy.

Santé
PROOST
Prost
SALUTE
Cheers

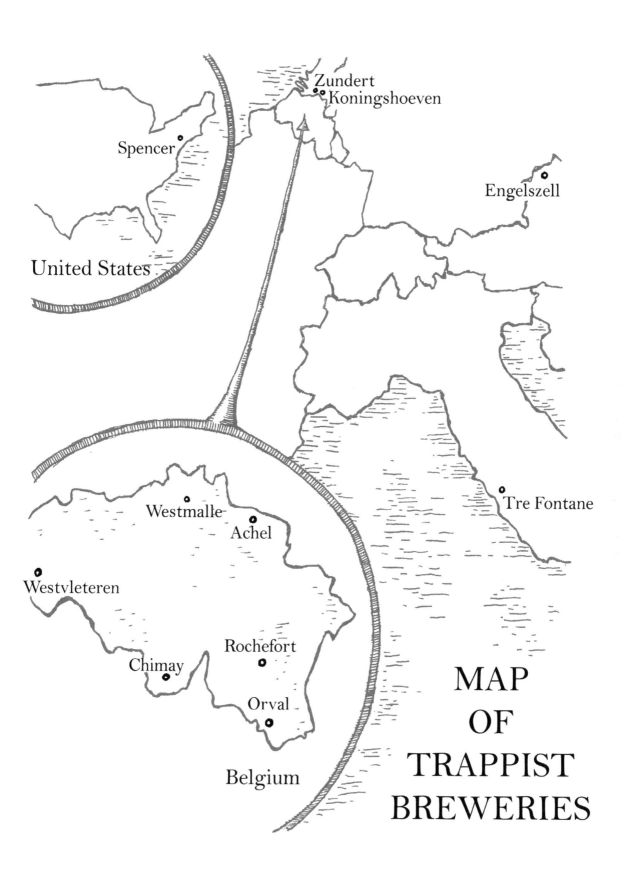

Zundert
Koningshoeven

Spencer

Engelszell

United States

Tre Fontane

Westmalle
Achel

Westvleteren

Rochefort

Chimay

Orval

Belgium

MAP
OF
TRAPPIST
BREWERIES

Illustrated map of the eleven Trappist breweries of the world. *Illustration by Jessica Deahl; source material courtesy of the International Trappist Association*

01. Trappist Origins

Saint Benedict immortalized in a fresco by Fra Angelico da Fiesole (circa 1437–1446). *The Yorck Project*

ORA ET LABORA:
THE RULE OF SAINT BENEDICT

Benedict of Nursia, now venerated by the Catholic Church as a patron saint of Europe, founded a monastery at Monte Cassino, Italy, in the sixth century. It was here he is believed to have written *Regula Benedicti*, or *The Rule of Saint Benedict*.

The text, which is divided into a prologue and seventy-three short chapters, serves as a mix of spiritual and administrative wisdom for monasteries. Known to be a reasonable and balanced work, Benedict's rule provides teachings about monastic virtues like humility, silence, and obedience while also providing practical directives for daily living (Theisen, 2015). In a broad sense, the rule is often summarized with the motto *ora et labora*, meaning "pray and work." While this rule was neither popular nor widespread during Benedict's lifetime, it would gain traction beginning in the Middle Ages and continues to inspire monastic communities around the globe today, including the Trappists. This bilateral philosophy is at the heart of why the Trappist monasteries covered in the upcoming chapters of this book brew beer to financially support themselves.

CISTERCIAN ORIGINS AT CÎTEAUX

"It all started in Cîteaux," Brother Benedikt Van Overstraeten succinctly says by way of our trusty interpreter Phil during an afternoon interview in a neatly appointed conference room at Westmalle Brewery. We have picked up pieces of Cistercian history at every abbey we've visited, but Brother Benedikt, particularly knowledgeable about the Order's early foundations, helped pull them together on a sunny June afternoon in Belgium.

From grain to glass, the Trappist beer you have wisely chosen to pair with your reading experience today has undergone a prodigious journey. Depending on the beer, the recipe itself could be months, years, decades, or even centuries old in origin. To fully appreciate the commitment, choices, and history that have shaped that beer, it is best to start by looking further back—much further back. Centuries before the Order of Cistercians of the Strict Observance—the order of Catholic monks commonly referred to as Trappists—was founded, a pivotal figure was already crafting a piece of spiritual wisdom that would inform the way the monks would live their lives.

There would not have been a Cîteaux without a monk named Robert, the abbot of a Benedictine abbey called Molesme in Burgundy, France. Molesme was originally founded on humble beginnings—a group of hermits—but it did not stay that way as its reputation grew:

> Members of the noblest families, hearing of the saintly lives of these religious [monks at Molesme], soon hastened from all parts of the country to join them, bringing in many cases their worldly possessions, which, added to numerous other benefactions, enabled them to erect a church, the most beautiful in the country around, and suitable monastic buildings. The increase in numbers and possessions caused a temporary relaxation in fervour, in so far that the monks ceased to relish the work of the fields, being willing to live on the alms given them. (Obrecht, 1911)

Frustrated by the lack of austerity being displayed by the monks at Molesme and eager to live a more secluded life, Robert set out to found a new monastery that would adhere to a much more literal interpretation of the Rule of Saint Benedict. In 1098, Robert, along with twenty-one of his most devoted monks, left Molesme to establish a new monastery in some marshy wilds around twelve-and-a-half miles south of Dijon.

"At first, the monastery was known simply as the 'new monastery,' but eventually took the name of the property, Cistercium or Cîteaux, which, in turn, gave rise to the name of the Cistercian Order itself" (*Our History: Cistercian Beginnings*).

According to *The Cistercian World, Monastic Writings of the Twelfth Century*, "Here they found that 'howling waste of a wilderness' through which God led his people after their escape from slavery in Egypt. The Community's experience of living out the exodus in all its rigour proved no less searching than the Israelites', and manna was not as once forthcoming" (Matarasso, 2006).

Cîteaux began as a community of great poverty. In its early days the monks set about

The Abbey of Cîteaux in modern times. *G CHP, ShareAlike 2.5*

constructing sleeping quarters and making the inhospitable land fertile for farming while using a nearby chapel as their place of worship until they could build a church of their own. The monks' days were devoted to not only prayer but a balance of manual labor, study, and contemplation, and the remote location of their new community all but removed them from the urban and feudal trappings of twelfth century Europe (*History of Christianity*, 2013).

Robert and his monks had only been at Cîteaux for a short time when the Molesme Community obtained a papal order from Pope Urban II to recall him to Molesme to resume his role as abbot. At least half of the brothers of Cîteaux joined him, returning to what some Cistercian chroniclers likened, in the spirit of ongoing metaphor, to a return to "the fleshpots of Egypt" (Matarasso, 2006).

The Prior of Cîteaux, a French monk named Alberic, was elected to succeed Robert as the second abbot of the remaining monks. Alberic continued Robert's commitment to austerity and humble poverty.

According to the *Penguin Dictionary of Saints*, when Alberic died, the English monk Stephen Harding, who would succeed him as the third abbot of Cîteaux, told the brothers, "You have lost a revered father and spiritual guide; I have lost, not only a father and guide, but a friend and fellow soldier of the Lord. . .who carried us all in his heart with affectionate love" (Attwater and John, 1995).

Harding was elected abbot in 1109, leading a small flock of remaining monks after the community was threatened by illness. One of his most substantial contributions to the then fledgling community was allegedly penning "Carta Caritatis" ("The Charter of Charity"). Through this document Harding "set the foundations of a decentralized monastic order, governed by a general chapter of abbots and characterized by mutual support, unity, and charity" (*Foundation and Expansion*). Unlike the monks at Molesme—and many other monasteries of the day and preceding it—Harding refused all gifts of wealth and land to the monastery, insisting the monks live and work in service of God through humble poverty. Needless to say, this rigorous lifestyle wasn't exactly attractive to wealthy, fickle would-be brothers; as a result few prospective new monks came to Cîteaux.

So it was a memorable day indeed when around the year 1112 or 1113 a Frenchman named Bernard arrived at Cîteaux on horseback, accompanied by a riding party of thirty relatives, all of whom were allegedly so taken with Bernard's testimony they had followed him to join the community of devoted monks. After just three short years in Cîteaux, Bernard, under the direction of Stephen Harding, would go on to found one of Cîteaux's greatest daughter houses, the Abbey of Clairvaux, in Ville-sous-la-Ferté, France. The achievement would become inseparable with Bernard's name and legacy.

Throughout his lifetime Bernard of Clairvaux developed a prominent reputation for being a gifted writer, captivating orator, and the primary builder of the Cistercian Order. Under his leadership men were dispatched to start 65 houses, while brother abbots started another 235. By the year 1200 there are said to have been more than 500 Cistercian houses in operation, growing to 742 by the eve of the Reformation (Pennington, 2005). It was quite a remarkable achievement for this austere order that took root in an inhospitable, wooded thicket.

The pivotal figures who helped shape Cistercian history during this first century have not been forgotten: today Robert of Molesme, Alberic of Cîteaux, Stephen Harding, and Bernard of Clairvaux are all honored as saints by the Catholic Church.

TRAPPIST REFORM IN THE SEVENTEENTH CENTURY

Today the famous Abbey of Notre Dame de la Grande Trappe is an easy eighty-four mile drive from Paris along a well-traveled thoroughfare, but for centuries the abbey, which was originally constructed as a small oratory chapel to the Virgin Mary in 1122, sat isolated in an idyllic valley nestled by forests and flowing streams. At first the monastery belonged to the Savigniac Order, but by 1147, the monks united with the Cistercian Order, and La Trappe, now elevated to the status of abbey, became directly subordinate to the abbot of Clairvaux. Over the centuries La Trappe suffered the dire effects of the Hundred Years War and from a lack of leadership under a series of absentee abbots. These were obstacles many of the other Cistercian abbeys in Europe also faced over time, and as a result many abbeys practiced less strict lifestyles than those led centuries before at Cîteaux.

By 1664, La Trappe had formally installed its most influential abbot to date: Armand Jean le Bouthillier de Rancé, a man who actually inherited the honorary title from his wealthy family more than twenty-five years earlier at the tender age of eleven (*A Newcomer's Guide to the Trappists*). In the wake of a series of tragedies culminating in his alleged participation in the 1660 death of the Duke of Orléans, de Rancé decided to renounce the vanities of life, along with all of his worldly possessions—except for the abbey—and retire to a more austere life. As abbot he preached a vegetarian lifestyle and "renewed the practice of monastic enclosure,

The Abbey of Notre Dame de la Grande Trappe. *P.Y. Stucki*

silence, and manual labor, expressing a spirit of apartness from all worldliness and a dedication to prayer and penance" (Pennington, 2005).

Under de Rancé's abbotship, Pope Alexander VII recognized within the Cistercian Order two observances: the Common and the Strict. From that point forward, as a nod to La Trappe, monks under the Order of Cistercians of the Strict Observance (OCSO) became known as Trappists and nuns under the same order became known as Trappistines. Practitioners of the common order remained known as simply Cistercians.

TRAPPIST STRUCTURE IN MODERN TIMES

Today there are around 175 Trappist and Trappistine monasteries worldwide, a number that has grown substantially since 1940, when there were just 82. Many of these new communities have formed in parts of the world where Trappists previously had little presence, namely Africa, Latin America, Asia, and the Pacific. While the total number of monasteries may be on the rise, the number of monks and nuns residing within them has paradoxically been on a steady decline over the same time period, as older communities age. Currently the average number of monks or nuns residing at any monastery is only twenty-three (and on our journey we observed many with far less); this is less than half of the average from previous centuries (*Who We Are*, 2010).

As the Trappists face the realities of a changing world, it is Stephen Harding's seminal document *The Charter of Charity* that still guides the Order's worldwide structure: "In accordance with the Charter of Charity,

Traditional Trappist architecture at Abdij Maria Toevlucht, Zundert, Netherlands. *Caroline Wallace*

Cistercian Communities are autonomous but united in a communion implemented by the institutions of the Father Immediate, the Regular Visitation, and the General Chapter" (*Who We Are*, 2010).

The Father Immediate is always the abbot of another monastery; assigned responsibilities include making a formal visit to the given community every two years. Known as the "Regular Visitation," the purpose of the Father Immediate's visit is "to strengthen and supplement the pastoral action of the local superior, to correct where necessary, and to renew the nuns' or monks' spiritual fervor" (*Who We Are*, 2010).

The General Chapter is considered the "supreme authority" in the Order, composed of the superiors of all the houses of monks and nuns worldwide. It meets every three years in the spirit of peace and charity to make decisions about maintaining the Order's unity and heritage, and is tasked with electing an Abbot General who serves an indefinite term, acting as a bond of unity. Assisting the Abbot General is a permanent council of five members who reside in Rome. The diverse council aims to represent the main language groups spoken by various communities within the Order (*Who We Are*, 2010).

Within the governance of the Trappist Order there are also a variety of commissions. The Central Commission is tasked with preparing the General Chapter. The Central Commission is elected by the previous chapter, and its members are chosen by the Order's various regions. There are other commissions that hold various functions from law to finance. The Trappists cite this practical structure as the foundation of the Order's growth. "From the very beginning the growth of the Order has been assured by a judicious system of foundations, governed at present by the Statute on Foundations. This statute has proven helpful in alerting Communities to the indications of Providence that they are invited to extend monastic life to other places, for example to such diverse localities as Norway, Syria and Brazil" (*Who We Are*, 2010).

At each Trappist monastery or abbey an elected superior oversees a community of brothers or sisters. The members of a community can come from diverse backgrounds. Some grow up in towns adjacent to the monasteries, while others travel from different regions of the world to join a particular community. Some become monks or nuns in their late teens or early twenties, while others are increasingly pursuing advanced education or careers in a variety of fields before following the spiritual call later in life. Sometimes these backgrounds end up informing the work they do in their monastic communities, from a former professional musician who continues to play his instrument for fellow brothers to a one-time structural engineer who uses his knowledge to oversee renovation work to the monastery.

In addition to the brothers or sisters, a Trappist monastery may also have laypeople employed in a variety of facets; often their work supports the economic activities of the monasteries. Because the monks' days are broken up with many different periods of prayer, these employees are integral to running abbey shops and cafés, assisting with labor (i.e., landscaping), and working under the monks' supervision in creameries, bakeries, distilleries, and breweries. Laypeople have been working alongside monks in monasteries for centuries, but as a diverse portfolio of revenue streams becomes increasingly necessary for monks to continue their way of life, there are more opportunities for ordinary citizens to find work at the monasteries.

TRAPPIST MONKS AND BEER

Many people, especially some of our fellow Americans, find it puzzling that men of such a serious faith commitment would brew, as well as consume, a beverage that is so often associated with sin and societal ills. The monks are quick to point out brewing was undertaken to make water potable before the advent of modern water treatment systems. Moreover, in European culture beer is a food—some monks look at it as "liquid bread." For these practical reasons the use of alcohol has never been so stigmatized in Europe; in fact, alcohol in the form of wine has long been associated with religious rituals (e.g., the Christian Eucharist).

While the Trappists may be the most well known order of monks brewing beer today, they were not the first. Ties between monasticism and the act of brewing beer go back centuries before the Order's foundations. According to *Brew Like a Monk: Trappist, Abbey and Strong Belgian Ales and How to Brew Them* (Hieronymus, 2005), as early as 750 AD, Charlemagne and his followers promoted the Benedictine way of life and brewing at monasteries. Later the Plan of Saint Gall, a highly treasured architectural drawing for a medieval monastery in Switzerland dating from around 820 AD, included plans for a brewery inside the monastic compound.

But why did the monks begin to brew? Beer's early popularity as a beverage is commonly—though not without historical dispute—attributed to the idea that prior to the rise of sanitation, beer was more potable than water. Yet many monks we spoke to told us the chief reason Trappists brewed beer in the early centuries was its nourishing properties. To supplement their meager diets, beer was a hearty beverage that would fill the stomach and provide some extra calories and nutrients—hence "liquid bread."

The monks' beliefs about beer's health benefits seem to be consistent with many modern scientific findings. According to Charlie Bamforth, professor of brewing sciences at the University of California, Davis, beer contains a significant amount of protein, as well as some fiber. His research has shown that beer is also a much better source for selenium, B vitamins, phosphorus, folate, and niacin than other alcoholic beverages (Bland, 2015).

Aside from its dietary role, beer served an important cultural and social function in early European life, and it was common for monasteries to have beer on hand for road-weary travelers who relied on monasteries for a warm bed, a hospitable meal, and a friendly brew while passing through these often rural areas. The monks, and laypeople who worked alongside them in the monasteries, tended to produce just enough beer to be consumed by the community and its guests, with no surplus available for sale or distribution far beyond their walls. All of that started to change on June 1, 1861, when Westmalle Abbey recorded its first commercial sale of beer. For a handful of Trappist monasteries beer would soon become a vital economic activity.

For each monastery, the beer or beers it chooses to brew hold a piece of its identity. It would be a misconception to think that Trappist beer is a style of beer all its own, because throughout history Trappist breweries have created a wide array of different brews, from Belgian table beers to Dubbels, Tripels, Quads, and inventive style-bending beers using native herbs, honey, and other adjuncts. The term Trappist serves as a designation and certification of origin.

THE INTERNATIONAL TRAPPIST ASSOCIATION AND AUTHENTIC TRAPPIST PRODUCTS

Thanks to growing distribution, by the twentieth century monks had developed a reputation all over the world for their highly sought after quality products, and for perhaps no line of products was this more true than for Trappist beers. With this increased notoriety came the opportunity for secular breweries to capitalize on consumer demand and fascination. With a host of beer labels featuring cheeky monks with a goblet in hand, it became difficult for consumers to differentiate between these "abbey beers" and authentic Trappist beers. It was nearly impossible to discern which beers were brewed at Trappist monasteries, as opposed to the abbeys of other religious orders. Moreover, consumers could not filter out beers produced by plain ol' commercial breweries hoping to pay a misguided homage to the monastic tradition, or worse, companies set on cashing in on a lucrative trend.

A case of Westvleteren beer bears the Authentic Trappist Product mark. *Caroline Wallace*

It was this market confusion, as well as the need to continue this important source of income for the monasteries, that drove some Trappist abbeys to start taking measures to protect their name. According to the International Trappist Association, Orval Abbey was the first to retain a lawyer: Since the name "Trappist" referred to the origin of the product, any businesses which subsequently and unjustly made use of the name "Trappist" or "Trappist Beer" could be sued for dishonest business practices. On September 6, 1985, the commercial court in Brussels made it even more explicit: "It is now common knowledge that customers attribute special standards of quality to products made by monastic Communities, and this is especially true of Trappist monasteries" (*Protecting the Trappist Name*). These legal protections for Trappist beers resulted in the rise of the term "abbey beer" as a catch-all to describe beers brewed at non-Trappist monasteries, or Belgian or monk-inspired beers sold by secular breweries.

As an extension of these legal endeavors, the International Trappist Association (ITA) was officially founded in 1996, and along with it came the introduction of the trademarked "Authentic Trappist Product" (ATP) label that could only be applied to goods from Trappist and Trappistine monasteries that met certain stringent requirements, depending on the product. Consumers could now be assured that if the beers, cheeses, chocolates, liquors, bread, honey, etc. they purchased bore this mark, they were indeed created by one of the monasteries. Eight Trappist breweries, including Belgium's Orval, Chimay, Westvleteren, Rochefort, Westmalle, and Achel; the Netherlands' Koningshoeven (La Trappe); and Germany's Mariawald became International Trappist Association members in the early days.

Before Trappist monasteries can place the Authentic Trappist Product mark on their products, they have to first and foremost satisfy three strict ITA criteria:

01. The product must be produced within the walls of a Trappist monastery, either by the monks themselves or under their supervision.
02. The factory must be of secondary importance within the monastery, and it should witness to the business practices proper to a monastic way of life.
03. The factory is not intended to be a profit-making venture. The income covers the living expenses of the monks and the maintenance of the buildings and grounds. Whatever remains is donated to charity for social work to help people in need or is used to support other abbeys. (*Products: Trappist Beers*)

Additionally, Authentic Trappist Products are required to meet rigorous health and safety standards, and their labels and advertising must be faithful to the modesty and austerity of the religious order. As a result, Trappist beer labels tend to be simple and typographically driven, refraining from featuring images of monks gobbling down a goblet of beer. Assuming all of these requirements are adhered to, it is still a lengthy process for a Trappist monastery to obtain ATP status for its beers. A monastery must first become a member of the International Trappist Association, at which point it will then be permitted to submit an application for the right to use the ATP mark on one of its products. Then the ITA chairman and board of directors will begin an evaluation process that can last several months and includes an on-site visit to check that correct procedures are being followed and that the product meets quality and taste standards. If the brewery is granted the right to use the ATP mark on its products, they must continue to meet these standards and will be subject to reevaluation every five years.

Today there are twenty monasteries who are members of the International Trappist Association, eleven of which brew beer. The pages that follow will tell the stories of these eleven.

The members of the
International Trappist Association
and the products they manufacture and/or sell

	trappists	trappistines	beer	cheese	wine/liquors	bread/biscuits	mushrooms	chocolate	honey/jam	oil	meat	yeast tablets	cosmetics	cleaning products	liturgical objects	others
Achel	●		✗													
Brecht		●											●	●	●	●
Brialmont		●					●								●	
Cardeña	●				●											
Clairefontaine		●				●										●
Echt-Tegelen	●										●					
Engelszell	●		✗	●	✗											
Klaarland		●				●			●			●			●	●
Koningshoeven	●		✗	✗		✗		✗	✗							
Mariawald	●			●									●			●
Mont des Cats	●		●	✗												
Orval	●		✗	✗					●							
Rochefort	●		✗													
Scourmont Lez Chimay	●		✗	✗												
Soleilmont		●				●									●	●
Spencer	●		✗						●						●	
Tre Fontane	●		✗		●			●		●						
Westmalle	●		✗	✗												
Westvleteren	●		✗													
Zundert	●		✗													●

✗ denotes Authentic Trappist Product

Chart detailing the wares of all twenty International Trappist Association members.
Illustration by Jessica Deahl; source material courtesy of the International Trappist Association

ORVAL

Abbaye Notre-Dame d'Orval (Orval Abbey)
Orval Brewery
Villers-devant-Orval, Belgium

Orval illustration. *Jessica Deahl*

02. Orval

Abbaye Notre-Dame d'Orval (Orval Abbey)
Orval Brewery
Villers-devant-Orval, Belgium

Rolling through the lush Belgian countryside—singing along with "Semi-Charmed Life" and other equally embarrassing road trip songs—we are three American women whose love of fermentation has taken us to some of the most coveted beer-producing facilities on earth. Following months of planning and coordination we have traveled thousands of miles to experience each of the world's Trappist breweries firsthand.

There is something especially awe inspiring about the enchanting serenity and impressive scale of Abbaye Notre-Dame d'Orval, or as it is known in our simplistic English tongue, Orval Abbey. As this is the very first Trappist brewery we visit on our journey, the iconic exterior of the abbey only seems to feed the swarm of nervous and excited butterflies swooping around in our

stomachs. As soon as our French interpreter Océane arrives, we all convene in an upstairs office to talk with Orval Brewery's General Director Philippe Henroz, along with Brother Xavier Frisque, chairman of the International Trappist Association and chairman of the board at Orval. The two men patiently and graciously tell us all about the abbey's history; then lead us on tours of the brewery and the monastery's grounds.

For visitors willing to make the remote drive to Villers-devant-Orval in the quaint municipality of Florenville—in the province of Luxembourg, part of Belgium's Gaume region—Orval offers far more public activities than the average Trappist abbey. While the brewery is only open for visitors to tour on a couple of "Open Door Days" per year (usually held in the fall), guests can enjoy food and

Orval Abbey. *Caroline Wallace*

Artifacts at Orval's monastic museum. *Caroline Wallace*

Artifacts at Orval's monastic museum. *Caroline Wallace*

drink at the À l'Ange Gardien restaurant, as well as visit Orval's monastic museum and abbey shop, and take walks alongside a garden of medicinal plants and on the trails of the natural reserve surrounding the abbey. For fans of architecture and history, it is Orval's large complex of historical monastic ruins which sit alongside the present day abbey that really make it a must visit.

It is not in history, but in legend where Orval's story really begins.

A STORIED PAST

According to local lore, Matilde (sometimes known as Matilda) of Tuscany—a legendary Italian feudal ruler who lived from 1046 to 1115 AD—was spending some time in this little patch of forest when she accidentally dropped her wedding ring into the sparkling spring that flowed from beneath the property. Desperate and frantic, she prayed for its return. To her amazement a trout then conveniently arose from the water carrying the ring in its mouth. Upon witnessing this miracle, Matilde is said to have cried out, "Truly this place is a Val d'Or (golden

valley)," and the name Orval was derived from the phrase. In her gratitude, Matilde was apparently inspired to start a monastery on these grounds. Today the spring remains the water source for the Orval Brewery, and the beer's label evokes this legendary tale.

"The first secret to making beer is the quality of the water," Brother Xavier says in eloquent French after sharing this legend with us.

We nod as Océane translates.

The first monks to settle at Orval arrived in 1070, a full twenty-eight years prior to the origins of the Cistercian Order at Cîteaux. These original monastic settlers were Benedictine monks from Calabria, in southern Italy, and they were welcomed not by Matilde, but by Count Arnould of nearby Chiny, who granted them the land. Upon their arrival the monks immediately began construction of a church and accompanying conventual buildings. Here they lived and worshiped for around forty years before mysteriously departing for reasons that have since been lost to history. After the Benedictines abandoned Orval, Count Arnould's son Othon

Today visitors can catch a glimpse of Orval's legendary spring waters in this small fountain. *Jessica Deahl*

invited a small community of Canons (a group of clergy who lived together in a common house, not unlike monks) to move to Orval and finish the remaining construction. The church was completed and consecrated in 1124, but the Canons ran into some financial trouble soon thereafter. Strapped for cash, the Canons sought to join the ranks of the Order of Cîteaux, as the Cistercians were in a period of great expansion during the time of Bernard of Clairvaux. Saint Bernard approved the Canon's request for affiliation, and in 1132, seven monks from the eldest of his daughter houses, the Abbey of Trois-Fontaines in Champagne, France, arrived in Orval to form a single community with the Canons. For Orval to truly be a Cistercian monastery the buildings needed to be altered to suit their specific worship practices, so construction began; the new church was completed by the end of the twelfth century (*A Long History*, 2011).

In its early existence under the Cistercian Order, Orval was economically sustained by farming, forestry, and iron works on lands adjacent to or in the region surrounding the monastery. These ventures led to prosperity, but the community faced devastation in 1252 when a pernicious fire left the abbey in ruins. Some of the buildings had to be reconstructed from the ground up, which was a difficult financial and spiritual burden on the community. This was Orval's first major setback as a Cistercian Community, but certainly not its last.

During the fifteenth and sixteenth centuries, as war between France and Burgundy ravaged the Gaume region, the abbey suffered extensive damage. In what Cistercians called an act of kindness, Emperor Charles-Quint allowed a foundry to be set up on the abbey's land to help pay for the repairs. The nave (central section) of the church also underwent construction during this time and was rededicated in 1533, with the community's twenty-four members present. As the sixteenth century turned into the seventeenth, Orval entered a high point for development under the leadership of an influential abbot. Bernard de Montgaillard was appointed abbot by Archduke Albert and

Archduchess Isabelle rather than by the community—a bold move that was originally not so popular. According to Orval's history,

> From that moment he devoted himself to his monks who finally became very attached to him. He put the monastery back on its feet economically and restored the buildings. But more especially he was a precursor in giving his Community reform constitutions which led to an increase in fervour. Novices came in great numbers; in 1619 the Community was composed of 43 members: 27 professed monks, 8 lay brothers and 8 novices. (*Spiritual Heights and Depths*, 2011)

During the Thirty Years War Orval faced its next destructive event at the hands of the troops of the Maréchal de Châtillon, who pillaged the monastery in 1637. The monks would again go into a period of reconstruction that would last through the end of the 1600s. During this time Orval had another important Abbot, Charles de Bentzeradt, who presided over the community 1668–1707. De Bentzeradt, like La Trappe's Armand Jean le Bouthillier de Rancé, was a reformer who led the Orval Community to take its place among the newly separate Order of Cistercians of the Strict Observance (Trappists, though it has been said Orval reverted to the common observance in 1785). The abbey was economically prosperous throughout the 1700s with its agricultural and industrial activities, and a fine new church designed by the famous architect Laurent-Benoit Dewez was consecrated in 1782 to hold the growing community.

This time of prosperity and celebration was cut short in 1789 as the French Revolution broke out, and Orval's position along the French border made it a vulnerable and immediate target. On June 23, 1793, revolutionary troops under the command of French General Louis Henri Loison plundered and burned Orval to ruins. The monks sought refuge in Luxembourg, then at Orval's daughter priory Conques—around fifteen miles north of the abbey—but the community was officially disbanded on November 7, 1795.

Orval's impressive medieval monastic ruins. *Caroline Wallace*

The entrance to the maze of ruins. *Caroline Wallace*

A well-preserved chamber. *Souvaroff*

The ruins tower to impressive heights. *Caroline Wallace*

The present day abbey through a medieval arch. *Jessica Deahl*

Orval's iconic Virgin and Child facade seen alongside the medieval ruins. *Caroline Wallace*

A characteristically monastic corridor. *Caroline Wallace*

"For more than a century the charred walls of Orval were at the mercy of the weather and of stone—and treasure—seekers" (*Spiritual Heights and Depths*, 2011). The once great Orval Abbey would have likely faded into the dusty scrolls of history if it were not for the de Harenne family, who eventually came to own the land containing its ruins. In 1926 the family made the generous decision to offer the plot back to the Cistercian Order so a new generation of monks could rebuild, live, and worship on these sacred grounds. A small group of monks was sent to form the first community, and Dom Marie-Albert van der Cruyssen from Ghent, Belgium, became its first abbot. Under his guidance a new abbey was built on the foundation of the eighteenth century monastery according to architect Henry Vaes's plans. (Vaes is also responsible for the design of the Orval glass.) According to *Cistercian Sites of Europe*, Vaes designed the church in the traditional Cistercian style, but drew some inspiration from Romanesque and art deco architecture. Construction was complete in 1948, and Dom Marie-Albert resigned his role as Abbot soon thereafter (*Resurrection*, 2011). Vaes's design, which features the unmistakable image of the Virgin and Child on the abbey's monumental facade, is today synonymous with Orval's visual and spiritual identity.

SAVED BY THE BREW

While some historical evidence suggests beer has probably always been brewed at Orval for the monks' consumption, commercial brewing officially began at Orval in 1931, to fulfill the economic role previously occupied by the foundry. Brother Xavier tells us beer played an

Barrels of Orval beer on display with reconstruction of the church seen in the background taken circa 1932–1936.

Courtesy of Orval Abbey

The Orval Brewery circa 1932–1936. *Courtesy of Orval Abbey*

An Orval delivery truck in 1937. *Courtesy of Orval Abbey*

integral role in the reconstruction of the monastery, but the work of brewing it did not fall on the monks, who were already busy producing bread and cheese for the community.

While the monks did, and still do, oversee beer production, the day-to-day brewing, cellaring, and bottling work at Orval has always been carried out by laypeople employed by the community. The origins of the distinct Orval recipe still produced today are said to go back to a handful of these laypeople: Orval's first Master Brewer, a German by the last name Pappenheimer (whose first name was Martin or Hans, depending on who you talk to), and Belgians Honoré Van Zande and John Vanhuele, who worked alongside him in the brewery during its first decade. These men used their diverse brewing backgrounds to craft a beer the world had never seen before. Vanhuele lived

in England for several years before coming to work at Orval, so he is credited with Orval's continued method of infusion brewing and the idea to dry hop the beer. The beer is still made with aromatic German and Slovenian hops that create a signature aroma, barley malted in Belgium, and a splash of liquid candy sugar that is traditional in many Belgian beers. Yeast is added after the brewing process to kick-start fermentation, and is again added prior to bottling, along with a second small dose of liquid candy sugar to initiate refermentation in the bottle.

Henroz takes us to see where the beer is made for ourselves. The showpiece brewhouse is where the magic starts; the incredible room, filled with a combination of five traditional copper and more modern copper lined kettles, along with whimsical stained glass and a ceiling of amazing lit-up stars, certainly looks the part.

Philippe Henroz shows the authors the underbelly of the brewhouse. *Caroline Wallace*

Br. Xavier Frisque posing in Orval's spectacular brewhouse. *Caroline Wallace*

"Here we do not speak of beer," Henroz says. But he is not saying this because this room is somehow too sacred a place to even utter the alcoholic beverage's name. He just means the yeast that turns the wort into beer is not added until the sugary liquid is transferred to the fermenters down in the belly of the brewery in a room below. Brewing just takes place on Mondays and Tuesdays at Orval, resulting in enough production to fill the six fermenters down here for the week. It helps that Orval only brews a single recipe (other than limited quantities of Green or "Petite" Orval), and Henroz does not see this changing anytime soon because demand is still very high. Focusing on a single beer lets the brewing staff utilize production time and space efficiently.

Down at the base of the fermenters we see the more industrial side of Orval; navigating the low ceilings, tight spaces, and winding passageways, it is easy to see why the brewery is not able to offer public tours aside from the rare "Open Door Days." Even listening to the recording from our tour with

Henroz, the conversation is blemished with interrupting calls of "Oops," "You go ahead," and "Careful, guys." Henroz explains that Orval's renovations and expansions over the years have had to be creative, if not piecemeal, because the brewery has to remain within the walls of the abbey. Water may continue to flow from Orval's generous spring despite seasonal change or a formidable draught, but space is not a renewable resource at Orval.

Where space does begin to feel more open again is in Orval's large bottling hall, a winding industrial marvel. As we admire its size and output capabilities, we are reminded when Orval first began brewing in the 1930s this space did not exist, so the beer had to be transferred to Brussels, where it was bottled at a different facility. Today fresh bottles, as well as sanitized recycled bottles returned to the brewery, whiz down the line at the rate of up to twenty-eight thousand 33 cL bottles per hour. After the bottling hall we enter Orval's cavernous cold storage area, climatized at 15°C (56°F). Here cases upon cases of beer sit piled to the ceiling for three to five weeks

Crates of Orval beer ready for delivery. *Caroline Wallace*

A glass of Orval served at À l'Ange Gardien. *Caroline Wallace*

while they undergo bottle refermentation. Soon these bottles will leave and go out for distribution for enjoyment all over the world.

Helming the team at Orval is Anne-Françoise Pypaert, the first female brewmaster a Trappist brewery has ever seen. As if Pypaert's resume is not impressive enough, she also leads the cheese-making program at Orval, and a giddy chance encounter with her during our tour really caps off the Orval experience.

THE BEER
Orval (6.2% ABV)

Orval, the namesake and sole true commercial output of the brewery, is a genre blending lightly colored beer with a frothy head and complex aroma influenced by dry hopping, along with the addition of Brettanomyces. When Orval is young the hops give it a fruity nose and a bite of bitterness. As Orval ages, the bitterness fades and the beer can develop a bright, slightly acidic character. Since Orval is a sediment-heavy beer, it is recommended those tasting it for the first time first enjoy a clean pour in appropriate glassware before

adding the yeast into the glass in the final sips for a whole different drinking experience.

TRAVEL TIPS

If you want to see inside the Orval Brewery you'll need to plan an autumn visit around the brewery's "Open Door Days." While the tour is free, it fills up quickly and advanced reservations are required. The rest of the year there are still plenty of reasons to visit Orval, including the opportunity to taste Green Orval (also known as Petite Orval), a 4.2% ABV beer originally brewed for just the monks and the guesthouse but now served at the À l'Ange Gardien restaurant just outside the abbey walls. Here you can also taste young and slightly aged Orval from the bottle or on draught and pair all of these fantastic beers with the cheeses produced at the abbey. There is also an abbey shop that sells bottles of beer to go, along with an impressive collection of books and an array of products made by other Trappist and Trappistine monasteries throughout Europe.

For a nominal fee visitors can explore the shop and attractions that lay beyond it on

View of Orval's monastic ruins through stained glass. *Jessica Deahl*

Orval's medicinal plant garden. *Caroline Wallace*

self-guided tours throughout the year and guided tours during summer months. A collection of pathways leads back past a garden of various medicinal plants, eye-catching sculptures, and the legendary spring where Matilde is said to have encountered the trout. Just beyond the spring, visitors can enter the monastic ruins and museum and get a clear sense of the size and scale of the former structures that occupied these hallowed grounds. Surrounding the abbey is an expansive nature preserve providing a couple different options for scenic strolls through picturesque scenery where glimpses of Orval's historic iron ore mining and forestry work can be seen. The nature reserve is home to a variety of animals, including grazing highland cattle and four different species of bats. Like all of the Trappist abbeys, Orval also has a guesthouse that welcomes individuals and groups for spiritual reflection and solitude rather than simply for beer tourism.

AREA ATTRACTIONS

Situated along the Belgian-French border, Orval is housed in some lovely countryside filled with historical significance, so anyone who is a fan of a good scenic drive would be remiss not visiting. For folks hopping from Trappist brewery to Trappist brewery, Chimay is less than two hours away and Rochefort is even closer, but does not allow visitors, as they do not have a shop or café.

A well-preserved tunnel leads to Orval's monastic museum. *Caroline Wallace*

Visitors to Orval's abbey shop may leave with as many as four cases of beer. *Caroline Wallace*

ACHEL

Saint Benedictus-Abbey—Achelse Kluis (Achel Abbey)
Brouwerij der St. Benedictusabdij de Achelse
Achel, Belgium

Achel illustration. *Jessica Deahl*

03. Achel

Saint Benedictus-Abbey—Achelse Kluis (Achel Abbey)
Brouwerij der St. Benedictusabdij de Achelse
Achel, Belgium

After spending the night in tech savvy Eindhoven, it is difficult for us to believe a remote Trappist monastery can exist in such close proximity to the hustle and bustle of this industrial region. There is too much noise, too many cars, and seemingly too much modernity for the likes of what we have seen at Orval and what we've painted as "Trappist" in our minds.

Moreover, the brewing operation is primarily run by a famous secular brewer named Marc Knops. The brewhouse is partially open for patrons of the on-premise café to view the brewing process. From our initial research it is far outside the realm of what Trappist breweries are like. As an early stop on our Trappist tour, though, we are open-minded about what the day will hold and excited to get a layperson's perspective on Monastic life.

Sint Benedictus Abdij De Achelse Kluis (Achel Abbey) is the smallest of the Belgian Trappist abbeys. It is situated along the border between the Netherlands and Belgium. A painted line denotes the boundary between the two countries about twenty feet in front of the main gate of the abbey.

Much to our surprise, despite the short thirty-minute drive from Eindhoven, the small town of Hamot-Achel is exceedingly quiet. It is situated in the middle of a large network of cycling and walking trails on a large nature preserve owned and maintained by the Dutch and Belgian governments since 1989.

The weather is ideal on the June morning of our interview, so we see several folks enjoying the outdoors as we near the monastery. The roads leading in are small and flanked on all sides by open fields and forestry thinned slightly for bike paths to weave through.

The gates of Achelse Kluis. *Caroline Wallace*

The brewhouse at Achel. *Caroline Wallace*

As we pull into the parking lot outside the abbey we note how empty it is. We have purposely scheduled our visit for a day when the café is closed, so this isn't overly surprising, but it is slightly intimidating. It feels as though it would be easier to shut us out with no one else around.

There is one other car in the lot, a bright green hatchback belonging to our interpreter, Filip. During our planning for the trip we came across Filip (or Phil, as he prefers to be called) through online craft beer forums. Like us, Phil is deeply interested in beer and is well established as a connoisseur throughout the region. He is a tall, strongly built man wearing a black coat, round-rimmed glasses, and a smart black cap on this brisk morning. He greets us with a firm handshake and a polite hello.

Phil has none of the reservations we initially showed. There is little that could intimidate him, and he has been to the abbey multiple times. His comfort with the area puts us at ease. From the start of our journey we had a self-perpetuating feeling that getting into these hallowed halls would be like breaking into Fort Knox. After all, two of the pillars of the Cistercians are solitude and silence. How could they possibly want to meet with us?

Phil assuredly walks around the perimeter of the abbey wall since the main entrance is locked when the café is closed. There is a driveway for trucks to pick up beers ready for distribution that we follow to a second entrance. We knock on the door and wait.

It takes several moments for an answer to come. We have time to check our itinerary with concern, confirm it is the correct date and time, and contemplate calling the resource who scheduled our meeting in an apologetic panic before a kind, middle-aged man opens the door for us. This is renowned brewer Marc Knops.

He ushers us into the brewhouse where his assistant brewer, Jordy Theuwen, is moving brewing equipment, and we make our introductions. Theuwen is younger than Knops and exudes an excited energy that puts us more at ease. Knops apologizes for keeping us waiting; he lost track of time and was busy at the kettles when we arrived.

That much is very clear to us, as the brewhouse is fully in action. The smell of boiling malt fills the air, and piping laces the wet floor below our feet. One of the things we love most about beer is the brewing process. There is a lovely balance struck in the act of brewing between the chemistry and the creative. That balance is universal, and if there is anyone we are going to meet who understands this, it is Knops.

We walk through the brewery while Knops matter-of-factly explains each step in his process. He is incredibly humble about the work he is doing despite his impressive résumé. He has been the head brewer of a number of other well known breweries in the region, like Brewery Domas in Leuven, but gives credit not to himself, but to the ingredients and the equipment. After the tour of the brewery we sit in the deserted café, drink the beers Knops and Theuwen are producing, and talk at length about life at Achel.

THE SECRETS OF THE KLUIS

St. Benedictus Abbey (Achelse Kluis) fell under the management of the Trappists in 1846, when twenty-seven monks from Westmalle Abbey set forth to establish the new community.

The buildings at Achel had stood for nearly two hundred years as a Catholic hermitage; Achelse Kluis translates to "The Hermitage of Achel." It was established as a priory in 1654, at the end of the Eighty Years War, as a refuge to respond to the exile of Catholics in the Netherlands. While that religious group was eradicated or disbanded by troops during the French Revolution, the tradition of contemplation, work, and prayer had been long established on the property, and the Trappists settled in very quickly in the mid-1800s.

By 1852, the brothers had established a farm, small dairy, and brewery on the premises. The community was growing and life was prosperous. Daughter houses had been established in Echt and Diepenveen in the Netherlands and in Rochefort, Belgium. In 1871 the priory was granted the status of abbey. In 1958 the brothers would go on to establish a priory in Kasanza, in the District Republic of the Congo.

Achel's courtyard is separated from the church and dormitories by this row of repurposed farm buildings. *Caroline Wallace*

One of the back entrances into the monks' dormitories and living quarters. *Caroline Wallace*

During World War II, the lines between the Netherlands and Belgium were delineated by miles of barbed-wire fencing. Part of that fencing has been reconstructed as a display for visitors at the abbey. *Caroline Wallace*

The early Achel Trappists brewed beer primarily to sustain themselves on a very regular schedule throughout the second half of the nineteenth century. They had two primary recipes: a light beer to take with their meals and a darker variation referred to as *patersvaatje* (the Achel patersbier).

World War I brought an immense change in life at Achel, as was the case with many other Trappist monasteries. The abbey was abandoned as war tore the area apart. In 1917 over 1,500 lbs of copper was stripped from the brewery by the Germans to provide armaments for the war effort. This plunder included the community's original copper brew system.

Tragedy for the area didn't cease outside the monastery's walls. On November 18, 1918, a week after the war's end was declared, a small fire lit by local children near the Hamont train station spread out of control, setting two German munition trains ablaze. When the fire reached the ammunition on board, an explosion so massive occurred that nearly two thousand

were reported dead or injured and Hamont was all but destroyed. The loss of life and destruction rocked the area to its core, and it took many years to recover.

REBIRTH IN THE MODERN AGE

It was not until after World War II that Trappists returned to Achelse Kluis. They rebuilt, expanding the monastery, and made their living growing vegetables and raising livestock as they had in the past.

As is the case with many Trappist monasteries, there was a real lack of novices coming into the abbey to adopt the lifestyle of a monk. The community was aging, and without a younger generation to replenish its vitality it would be impossible to continue sustaining the farm. A new vocation for earning income was needed.

In 1989 the community sold a large portion of its farmland to the Dutch National Forest Service. Using these funds while working closely with Westmalle Abbey, the community rebuilt its brewery in the renovated

Today, the line between Belgium and the Netherlands comes in the form of a painted line on the road toward Achel's gates. *Caroline Wallace*

"A tasty thirst-quencher, light but with a great taste; that is what the day trippers are after. A genuine, pure beer without added aromas," Brother Thomas said in an interview with famed beer writer Michael Jackson (2001).

The first beers to emerge from the Achel fermenters were the Achel Blond 5 and the Achel Bruin 5. Both beers are 5% ABV and serve as a refreshing drink after a day in the sun.

While Brother Thomas was known for his tenacity, he was also well into his seventies when he was recruited to be the consulting head brewer at Achel. To help carry the load and eventually to step in altogether, Achel reached out to Brother Antoine of Rochefort. He had been heading up the brewing practices there since the mid-1970s.

Under Brother Antoine's guidance the recipes were completed for the 8% ABV beer offerings Achel Blond 8 and Achel Bruin 8, as well as the Blond Extra and Bruin Extra, which come in at 9.5% ABV. These are Achel's offerings in the Dubbel and Tripel category, showcased with two different malt profiles.

barn and set to work finding individuals to brew on the system. If they could not farm anymore, the brothers would brew.

The first monk brewer brought in was Brother Thomas of Westmalle. He had played an integral role in the beer program there, so in 1998, he emerged from his vocational retirement at Westmalle and traveled to Achel. His first order of business was to establish a style that would meet the needs of patrons after a day on the trails.

One of Achel's two on-premise shops. *Caroline Wallace*

The serene courtyard outside the monks' primary living quarters. *Caroline Wallace*

This parity of having a light and dark beer representative at each break in alcohol content harkens back to the original brewing history of Achel, when they produced two beers of similar ABV percentage: one that was light and one that was dark. It is a very unique portfolio in the Trappist brewing world and one of which Achel is proud.

In 2001 Brother Antoine handed the reins of the brewery to secular headbrewer Knops. Knops has been well known throughout Belgian beer culture for over twenty years. He was head brewer at the famous brewery Domas in Leuven, Belgium, and contract brews throughout Europe to this day. He spends only a few days a week at Achel overseeing the production of beer and depends heavily on Theuwen to maintain order while he is abroad brewing on other breweries' systems.

In 2002 Jules Van den Bossche came to Achel to join the community. He worked closely with Knops for nearly twelve years, manning the brewery and interacting with patrons. In 2013, Brother Jules left the brotherhood. Knops' protégé Theuwen was ready to step in for Brother Jules as assistant brewer.

ACHEL TODAY

Theuwen has a history with the abbey longer than many outside of the monks; his mother has run the café since 1999. Theuwen has spent most of his adolescence and all of his adult life on the grounds of Achel, working in the café, tending to the grounds, or supporting Knops' brewing vision.

It is impossible to mistake the love Theuwen has for the abbey and the beer he produces. While we tour the monastery grounds, he shows us tiny details on the buildings he has found and studied over the decades. He tells their stories, speaking to us in a gentle whisper on the silent grounds out of respect for the brothers' privacy and peace.

He shows a similar reverence for the art of brewing. While we walk through the unusual Trappist brewery, it is clear he and Knops are proud of the unique features the abbey's brewhouse has to offer beer enthusiasts like us.

They have a dual-purpose kettle that serves as their mash tun and kettle, cutting out time and energy lost during the transfer of wort from one vessel to the other. A secondary vessel filters the spent grain from the wort prior to the boil and hop additions.

Marc Knops and Jordy Theuwen stand in front of the brewery's newest packaging facility. *Caroline Wallace*

The Trappist Achel 5 Bruin and Trappist Achel 5 Blond are stored and served from these tanks in the brewery's attic post-fermentation. *Caroline Wallace*

In terms of hops, Knops specifically opts for dried whole leaf hops. To him, the flavor and quality cannot be matched by any other alternative. Although we have seen other Trappists use hops in all shapes and forms, we can't help but comment on how fantastically fragrant the dried leaves smell comparatively as we make our way through the hop storage area.

The brewers have four fermenters where their beers go through active fermentation and a lagering period. The Bruin 5 and Blond 5 are piped into the attic post-fermentation to a pair of serving tanks that store the freshly made beer. These tanks' systems hook up directly to the bar's draft lines downstairs, and the beer is poured and carbonated as soon as a patron orders it, ensuring it is as fresh as possible.

The Blond 8, Bruin 8, Blond Extra, and Bruin Extra are all bottled in one of the brewery's two bottling facilities after a second addition of yeast and sugar. The 8-level beers and the Bruin Extra are then packaged for distributors. The Blond Extra and the 5-level beer are only available for sale on premises, so Blond bottles will not be crated for wider distribution, but rather moved to the café and abbey shop.

We spend far longer than our planned two hours talking with Knops, Theuwen, and Phil. The brewers graciously open bottles of Blond Extra from the cellars and pour us glasses of Blond 5 and Bruin 5. Our conversations move from Achel, to what styles we are drawn toward, to the differences in American and Belgian beer culture, to regretful tattoos people receive. Where we initially felt such apprehension in the emptiness, we now feel at ease and open.

The quiet when the café is closed alludes to something far sadder. The Community at Achel is incredibly small—only four brothers. Achel is an aging community, with the youngest being seventy-three at the time of our tour. It is difficult to draw younger monks to Achel because, as with any other society, to be the only young person in a group of people at an entirely different stage of life is isolating.

A view into the abbey from outside the gate. *Caroline Wallace*

This brings up a very real concern: What will happen to Achel's beer program when the monks are gone? The brewery would no longer meet the requirements set forth by the International Trappist Association to be called Trappist. Will Theuwen and Knops continue on as they have in the past, brewing abbey ales rather than Trappist? Could the world lose the Bruin 5 and the Blond Extra forever? It is yet unwritten, but the Community at Westmalle—Achel's mother abbey and Knops's point of contact for most business decisions regarding the beer program—is brainstorming mitigations to keep Achel as it has been for 150 years: Trappist and brewing.

THE BEER

Trappist Achel 5 Blond (5.00% ABV)

A light hay-colored Belgian blond ale, Achel 5 Blond is mildly spicy, with plenty of citrusy hops on the nose. It pours at the perfect temperature every time with a white foamy head, and it is only served at the Achel Café. This was one of the original recipes dreamed up by Brother Thomas of Westmalle Abbey when Achel began its beer-making pursuit in the mid-1990s, and is still one of the beers bringing in multitudes to the tasting room. With a medium-light body and floral, yeasty, almost herbaceous notes in the taste, it is a wonderful, sessionable ale.

Trappist Achel 5 Bruin (5.00% ABV)

The darker brother to the Achel 5 Blond, 5 Bruin pours a light brown shade with mahogany highlights. It smells of raisins, sweet caramel, and a touch of Belgian yeast. While it is darker, this 5.00% Bruin is as drinkable as its Blond counterpart, with a surprising medium light body and dark fruit taste. It is also only available on premise on draft.

Trappist Achel 8 Blond (8.00% ABV)

The Achel 8 Blond is similar to a Tripel style beer, but one that has a notable sense of balance and a dry finish compared to other Belgian Tripels. Grassy hops and white wine are in the nose, with plenty of traditional peppery notes behind them. It is medium-bodied and hides its formidable 8.00% ABV well. It tastes of oranges, apples, peppery spices, and yeast. Unlike the 5 Blond and Bruin, the Achel 8 Blond is available globally in 330 mL and 750 mL bottles.

Trappist Achel 8 Bruin (8.00% ABV)

Achel 8 Bruin is Achel's interpretation of a Belgian Dubbel. It has a beautiful ruby body with garnet highlights and a lower carbonation level than 8 Blond, lending to a silkier mouth feel. The nose is much heavier on the malt, with dark fruit, a slight citrus tang, and indication of its higher alcohol content. It tastes bready, with a nice transition from sweet to yeasty, to a very slight hop taste at the finish. Achel 8 Bruin is available globally in 330 mL and 750 mL bottles.

Achel Blond Extra (9.50% ABV)

The Achel Extra Blond is a special 9.50% ABV behemoth available for sale on draft and in 750 mL bottles. It recently went through a redesign of its label art and now features illustrations of the abbey and surrounding landscape. It pours a deep gold color with a billowy head that leaves a thick lacing. In the nose there are notes of yeast, clove, a little banana, and a slight hint of grass. It is medium bodied and balanced, even for its alcohol level. There is lots of yeast in the flavor, as well as banana and caramelized fruits, with a crisp hop taste and a clean crisp finish.

Achel Trappist Extra (9.50% ABV)

The darkest and biggest of Achel's offerings, Trappist Extra is sold globally in 330 mL and 750 mL bottles. It pours a dark brown color with red-orange highlights and a lush tan head. An aroma of malt, raisins, toffee, a little cocoa, and dark fruit drifts up from the glass. It has a rich sweet taste with notes of figs and malt, with plenty of esters and a touch of its 9.50% ABV.

A freshly poured glass of Trappist Achel Extra Blond. *Caroline Wallace*

Jordy Theuwen and Marc Knops sit enjoying their wares in Achel's tasting room. The brewhouse can be seen through a glass pane in the background. *Caroline Wallace*

TRAVEL TIPS

The abbey's café, artisanal grocery, and bookshop are open to visitors Tuesday through Saturday. Sundays the café and bookstore remain open but the grocery shuts its doors. Depending what time of year you choose to visit, the café's doors open at 11:00 a.m. or 12:00 p.m. to start pouring beer for thirsty patrons, including the Achel 5 Bruin and Achel 5 Blond—only available on draft— and the Achel Blond Extra, which is available on draft and in 750 mL bottles for takeaway sales. This is the only place to buy bottles of Blond Extra.

AREA ATTRACTIONS

There are robust hike and bike trails peppering the countryside just around Achel's gates. It is also a thirty-minute drive from the bustling tech city of Eindhoven, where there is plenty to explore in the town's center. If you are staying in the city, there are fabulous accommodations, including an excellent hostel called Blue Collar Hotel situated in a renovated lightbulb factory. With cool, industrial furnishings, kitschy fun touches, a great bar, and two wonderful restaurants serving breakfast, lunch, and dinner, it is easy to stay in after a day on the trails.

LA TRAPPE

Abdij Onze Lieve Vrouw van Koningshoeven
(Abbey of Our Lady of Koningshoeven)
La Trappe Brewery
Berkel-Enschot, Netherlands

La Trappe illustration. *Jessica Deahl*

04. La Trappe

Abdij Onze Lieve Vrouw van Koningshoeven (Abbey of Our Lady of Koningshoeven)
La Trappe Brewery
Berkel-Enschot, Netherlands

Just across the Dutch border, near the small city of Tilburg in the North Brabant region of the Netherlands is Koningshoeven Abbey. After a night in Eindhoven we crisscross the windmill-dotted countryside and approach the abbey. The scene is starting to become familiar: a tree-lined boulevard, seemingly far from modernity, leads us to a fortressed abbey immersed in unwavering antiquity. Despite the familiarity, we soon realize the "La Trappe" beers are as varied and forward-thinking as the abbey itself.

This morning we are scheduled to meet with current Prior of the Community Brother Isaac and Elske Vugts, who manages the abbey's marketing strategies. Now that we have visited a couple abbeys, we are beginning to understand that while each is bonded by its adherence to the Rule of Saint Benedict, they all have nuanced approaches to monastic life. Koningshoeven proves to be among the most modern and easily accessible of the abbeys we

visit. Linda, an instructor at a nearby university, joins us for the interview to act as interpreter, but we quickly discover both of our hosts speak excellent English. After a brief but warm greeting, Brother Isaac launches into his tour of the brewery and abbey grounds. With more than 150,000 visitors each year to Koningshoeven Abbey, it is apparent he is accustomed to providing interviews. La Trappe, compared to some of the other monastic breweries, is incredibly open to visitors. It boasts an operating abbey shop, tasting room, and scheduled brewery tours.

Brother Isaac is a statuesque and noble looking monk dressed in the traditional habit, with a bald head and small circular glasses. He is friendly and to the point. As we struggle to keep up with his assured gait, he stops for a moment to reach into his robe pocket and pull out an iPhone donned with a "La Trappe" branded phone case. This abbey is certainly not antiquated. With a focus on

The monastery at Koningshoeven Abbey. *Courtesy of Koningshoeven Abbey*

sustainability and responsibility, many of the buildings of the community feature solar panels to improve efficiency. A dynamic group of twenty-two monks live and work at the monastery, with jobs ranging from managing the new web store (their "e-monk") to running the abbey shop, making cheese, jam, and bread, and producing beer.

As expected, the abbey grounds are breathtaking. We walk through the compound of neo-Gothic buildings restored and upgraded with care. La Trappe's motto is "Taste the Silence," and it is a fitting one. Promotional material features the following adage:

> The most beautiful sound in the
>   world is silence.
> In silence you can listen to yourself
>   and to others.
> Silence is the sleep that
>   nourishes wisdom.
> Silence begins with attention and
>   what receives your attention
>   begins to grow.
> Silence is the white between
>   the written lines.
> In silence things intensify.

Time spent with one of La Trappe's beers is time for yourself. "We want silence in the glass, when you can have a moment of peace like a monk," Vugts says. Certainly, drinking one of La Trappe's wide variety of beers provides an opportune moment for contemplation and appreciation for the place it was made.

HISTORY OF OUR LADY OF KONINGSHOEVEN ABBEY

The story of Our Lady of Koningshoeven Abbey is largely that of the brewery. Heavily intertwined since the beginning, the abbey was established March 5, 1881, and the monks began to brew beer three years later. The brewery at Koningshoeven has been necessary for covering the costs of expensive developments and the continuation of monastic work at the abbey.

The Trappist monks, according to tradition, must live by the work of their hands. The strict observance of the Rule of Saint Benedict is the distinguishing element of the Trappist monks, and the importance of manual labor is a pivotal facet of this reform. The selection of appropriate monastic work must allow for a focus on God and time for reverie and reflection, and the avoidance of temptation and frivolity. Current Abbot of Koningshoeven Abbey Dom Bernardus describes in the preface to *Bier in Alle Eeuwigheid*, the "intrinsic tensions embedded in this rule. . .it shows clearly that this is a matter of finely tuned balancing, but also that it is possible. Mainly it shows that heaven and earth cannot do without one another." This lifestyle of prayer and work is not easy to maintain, and those challenges are evident in La Trappe's history.

The first Prior of the abbey, Nivardus Schweykart, was eager to find another source of income to help pay off debts the abbey had accrued. The son of a brewer from Munich, he saw the promise of sustainability and growth in developing a brewery at the abbey. In 1884 the Dutch province North Brabant had 174 operating breweries and a handful in Tilburg. Beer was a welcome alternative to polluted drinking water and had an important place in local culture. Ceremonial beers are common in the area to celebrate birth, death, and fairs (Sapens, 2009, 31). One surviving tradition is called *Pannenbier* (roof-tile beer), during which builders celebrate reaching the highest point of a new construction by sharing a few crates of beer with the future owners.

Sign for the La Trappe Tasting Room, where La Trappe's roster of beers can be sampled year-round. *Caroline Wallace*

Exterior view of the La Trappe brewery. *Caroline Wallace*

In February 1884 Nivardus Schweykart sent Brother Isidorus Laaber by train to Munich to learn to brew bottom-fermenting lager. Originating in the Czech town Pilsen around 1840, Pilsen beers (or lagers) were quickly gaining popularity. The Prior wanted to capitalize on this and saw an opportunity to market a new type of beer in the Netherlands. Producing Pilsner required refrigeration equipment, and the Koningshoeven monks were fortunate enough to have a steam-driven ice machine at their disposal. They were quite progressive from the start with the type of beer they produced and the brewing methods to do so.

In the first few years of its existence the brewery faced many difficulties. The facility had been set up on a limited budget and was unfortunately designed to produce top-fermenting ales, not the bottom-fermenting lagers Brother Isidorus had been training for. By the time he returned from Munich as an able lager brewer, he immediately realized the blunder and had to reformat the brewing equipment. They successfully brewed two beers in 1884 (about 1,700 barrels) under the name "De Schaapskooi" ("The Sheepfold") and sold their beers under the

The monastery at Koningshoeven Abbey. *Caroline Wallace*

registered name "Steam Brewery of the Trappist Fathers," which highlighted their up-to-date technology. The brewery's first customers were the property's landlords, and it wasn't long before they had export trade contracts in Belgium, France, and Great Britain.

In October 1888 the monks ordered their first batch of bottles, and with a premiere bottling line in operation they pioneered the processes of packaging De Schaapskooi beer. In 1892 the brewery even installed its first telephone line—among the first in the Netherlands to do so. A new steam engine meant they could generate electricity for the brewery, abbey, and the abbey church. Expanding the brewery meant more income which, as described in Benedictine doctrine, was cycled back into the church. The first abbot, Dom Willibrord Verbruggen, decided to build a new abbey as an "expression of the emancipation of the Catholics in the Netherlands" (Sapens, 2009, 56). The complex was built following a neo-Gothic style, and its design informed the formation of several monasteries in France, Belgium, and the United States.

The flourishing brewery fell victim to the Abbot Willibord Verbruggen's zeal and propensity to spend money faster than it was earned. After the abbot of Mont-des-Cats visited in 1906 and discovered serious debts, Abbot Verbruggen was asked to hand over the property. Eventually the pope discharged the abbot from office and the monks were asked to leave the monastery. Brewing continued on a very tight budget until it could no longer be sustained. When a new abbot was installed in October 1909 the monks moved back to the monastery in small groups and beer production gradually ramped up again. Output at the brewery has been dependent on the abbey's needs: increased to build or sustain the monastery and sized down again when demands are met (Sapens, 2009, 64).

World War II also had an effect on brewing production. With rationed ingredients De Schaapskooi actually expanded production to 17,000 barrels annually. It was obligatory that wartime beer contain smaller amounts of alcohol, so it was possible to produce a lot more with the same amount of

Sheep at Koningshoeven Abbey. In 1884, the abbey brewed beers under the name "The Sheepfold." *Courtesy of Koningshoeven Abbey*

ingredients. The occupying Germans also drank a significant amount of the malty beverage. Fortunately, the ravages of war and Nazi occupation had little effect on the abbey other than monetarily. This short-term increase in profits meant the abbey could pay off long-standing debts, but this small period of prosperity did not last long.

After the war the brewery was in a doleful state. Available brewing ingredients were scarce and of poor quality, and the equipment was in disrepair. The need for a major shift in the business structure of De Schaapskooi was becoming more and more apparent to the brothers.

Up to this point, beer was delivered to buyers around the abbey by an employed beer salesman. This man drove a horse and cart to all the local pubs and had a "sort of pictur-esque aura that fully fitted his occupation. His usually rather corpulent physical appearance was a result of the many beers he drank. It was part of his delivery job to taste one with every landlord" (Sapens, 2009, 114).

The Community at Koningshoeven had grown to support 150 brothers, and living from the proceeds of the farm alone was not sustainable. The monks, recognizing the importance of brewing to their financial well-being, made a critical step toward commercialization: in the 1950s they began brewing beer for the supermarket chain "De Spar," which increased production to a significantly larger capacity driven by the demand of the brothers' new contracts.

It was becoming common practice for Dutch breweries to broker contracts with local pubs that ensured barkeeps would serve their brews exclusively. Ergo, multiple versions of these contracts, referred to as "tied houses," existed in the Tilburg region during the mid-1900s. In fact, there were upwards of 135 Trappist pubs in the area serving only the beer produced by De Schaapskooi. The pub owners had to buy beer from De Schaapskooi, but also pay back the funds the abbey had loaned them to establish the Trappist pubs. It was not uncommon for landlords to default on these business loans from the abbey, calling on the

Proceeds from beer production funded construction of a new abbey completed in 1893. *Courtesy of Koningshoeven Abbey*

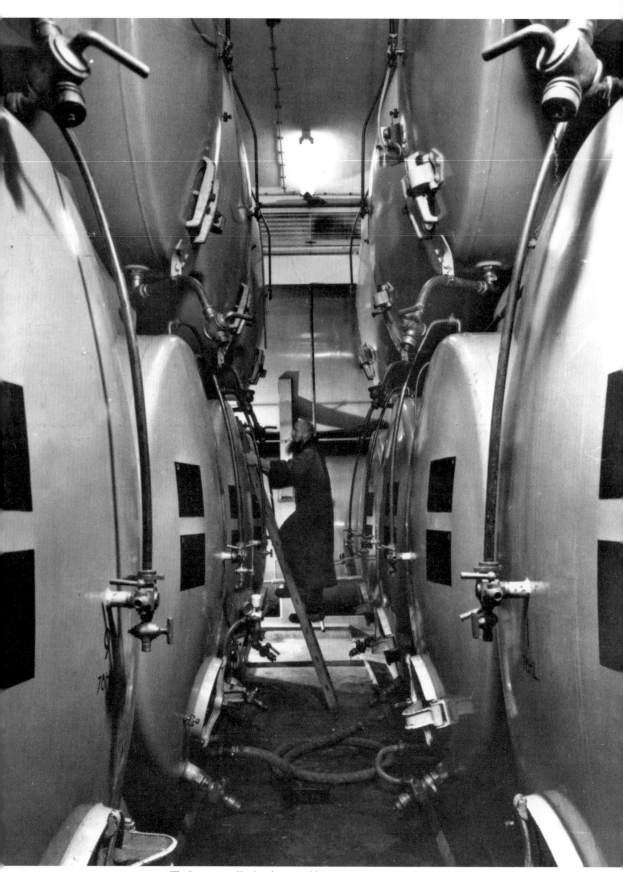

The brewery at Koningshoeven Abbey. *Courtesy of Koningshoeven Abbey*

monks' Christian charity as a means for exemption. This abuse of the community's values put the brothers in a difficult position professionally (Sapens, 2009, 115).

With the turn toward commercialization in the postwar years, the brewery thrived. While profits soared, the daily clamor of increased production began to take its toll on the monks. By 1969, 15 monks and 150 laymen worked in the brewery. The constant noise proved disruptive to a contemplative way of life. As financial demands increased the brewery had to produce more beer, and upping production meant more employees and increasing investments. The only way to curtail this distracting expansion was to make a drastic and systemic change, and on October 26, 1969, the decision was made to strike a deal with Artois, a private Belgian company. Though the monks were hopeful that with Artois at the helm of the abbey's brewing activities the brothers could maintain their peace while the community also maintained much-needed funding, this was not to be. Only a year after the agreement was made, just half of the brewery's production capacity was used and De Schaapskooi became progressively less profitable. By 1979, the brewery was no more than a "beer trading office" (Sapens, 2009, 126), and in April the contract between the abbey and Artois was terminated.

An influx of young monks in the 1970s reinvigorated the abbey. The dormant brewery was eventually revived on January 18, 1980, under the helm of Father Godfried Looijaard. Along with brother Eligius Martens and four employees, Looijaard worked tirelessly to rebuild. In its first year, the brewery's output was only 117 hL (100 barrels), but it had a significant meaning to the community—it was beer that once again belonged to the monks. As a marketing decision the resurrected brewery was equipped to produce top-fermenting ale, unlike the bottom-fermenting lagers that distinguished it in the past. By this time there was an enormous pool of lagers on the market in the Netherlands and Belgium, and the abbey wanted to be competitive. As a further distinction, the brewery produced bottle-conditioned ale.

The abbey also chose the name "La Trappe" to mark the brewery's new era and advertising policy. The name is a nod to the sixteenth century La Trappe monastery in Normandy, France, and was much easier to pronounce, opening the brand to an international market. A layman was hired to manage the brewery in the 1990s, the first non-monk they had trusted with this leadership role since the 1880s. With a new brand image and marketable specialty beers, the manager had his eye on the United States. La Trappe began producing a 10% ABV Quadrupel in addition to its Dubbel (7%) and Tripel (8%). The manager also launched a Single (Blond, 6%) to round out La Trappe's collection based on the refectory beers the monks drank during meals. La Trappe became the first brewery to market and sell its own table beer. Exports to the American market began in 1994.

A multimillion dollar renovation was necessary to boost production, and the abbey once again looked to the market for help. In 1997 they paired up with Bavaria, one of the

The monks at Koningshoeven Abbey embrace a spirit of giving. *Caroline Wallace*

The brewery at Koningshoeven Abbey. *Courtesy of Koningshoeven Abbey*

Exterior view of the old brewery. *Caroline Wallace*

Copper brewing vessels in the old brewery. *Courtesy of Koningshoeven Abbey*

Exterior view of La Trappe brewery, which implements solar panels for energy efficiency. *Caroline Wallace*

largest independent breweries in the Nether-lands. In an effort to not repeat failed business unions in the past, the monks were incredibly conservative about partnering with another company. Bavaria is a family business owned and operated by the Swinkels family since 1746. This was appealing to the monks at Koningshoeven, as the monastic community is also akin to a family. In March 1999, the Swinkels family and the abbey signed an agreement of cooperation, and all of the equipment and brewing activities belonged to Bavaria, while the abbey owned the rest of its operation, buildings, and the brand (Sapens, 2009, 190).

The International Trappist Association (ITA), through a series of authorizations, deems which products can don the much-re-nowned hexagonal logo on its labels. After La Trappe coupled with Bavaria, they had to "wage a fierce fight" to reacquire the distinc-tion (Sapens, 2009, 190). With some contract and business readjustment La Trappe was once again an Authentic Trappist Product in August 2005. The fluid landscape of the beer business has caused the ITA to evolve and adapt accordingly while still carefully protect-ing its mark. Reacquiring the logo proved very profitable for the brewery, and by 2005, Our Lady of Koningshoeven was able to

advance its export market, "which then grew steadily to 35% of its total volume in 2008" (Sapens, 2009, 191).

SUSTAINABILITY AND GIVING

Koningshoeven Abbey, fueled by profits from the brewery, has long embodied the spirit of giving and practice of caritas, or Christian love. After rebounding from the financial struggles of World War II, Koningshoeven was able to found two abbeys elsewhere: one in Indonesia (1955) and another in Kenya (1967). The abbey in Kenya was deserted in 2007 because of political instabilities, but a new monastery is currently being developed in Uganda. As we talk with Brother Isaac about these daughter houses, he admits there are difficulties fostering a monastic communi-ty abroad, and he personally visits Uganda often. The brothers at this monastery special-ize in agriculture and cattle breeding, and the money they earn is currently used to renovate local schools and provide safe drinking water to the community.

Supporting this abbey in Uganda has primarily been funded through the proceeds of the brewery, particularly due to the sales of the brewery's 125th anniversary beer. In addition to its efforts in other countries, the abbey also offers work to those with learning

La Trappe's branding evolution displayed in the abbey gift shop. *Caroline Wallace*

Inside the old brewery. *Caroline Wallace*

difficulties or mental disabilities in the local Tilburg Community. This community of monks truly has heart. People from the Prins Heerlijk and Diamant groups are offered jobs in housekeeping, gardening, and packing; catering establishments; or the monastery shop. Brother Isaac tells us psychiatric patients working to cultivate jam at the abbey have found a "new balance" in their life. The abbey provides a safe and quiet environment for work and rehabilitation, and the entire team becomes richer for its charitable work.

In addition to the importance of giving back at La Trappe, a forward-thinking approach toward social and environmental responsibility and sustainability has been implemented. Brother Isaac is proud of the efforts the community has made to limit environmental impact. A percentage of barley for the beer is sourced and grown locally, and the monks use spent grain from the brewery to bake bread at the abbey. The monastery has invested in solar power and electric vehicles for some necessary traveling, but the main effort is to keep economic activity as close to the source as possible.

Inside the old brewery. *Caroline Wallace*

An impressive brewhouse. *Caroline Wallace*

THE BEER

La Trappe PUUR (4.7% ABV, organic)

A sessionable, light ale brewed with entirely organic ingredients, it is a representation of La Trappe's continuous efforts toward sustainability and top quality beer. It is effervescent and lightly hopped while maintaining the character of the Belgian yeast.

La Trappe Witte Trappist (5.5% ABV)

La Trappe Witte is brewed with citrusy, aromatic Saphir hops. It pours a hazy yellow, with an effervescent and persistent head. The spicy, aromatic character defies the senses, as there are no added spices in the recipe. The world's first Trappist witbier is best served cold.

La Trappe Blond (6.5% ABV)

A well-balanced golden ale perfectly marries sweet malt with fresh and fruity characters. Slightly bitter at the finish, this unfiltered ale is full of Belgian yeast aroma and body.

La Trappe Dubbel (7% ABV)

La Trappe's Dubbel utilizes caramel malts for a deep ruby-brown color and rich, caramelly mouth feel. It is soft and fragrant on the nose and deceptively refreshing for its ABV.

La Trappe Isid'or (7.5% ABV)

Isid'or was brewed to celebrate Koningshoeven's 125th anniversary, modeled after Brother Isidorus's founding recipe. An unfiltered, bottle-conditioned amber ale, Isid'or features a slight caramel sweetness and a lingering fruity aftertaste. The label features a portrait of Isodorus, and the brewery's website describes it as a "top-fermenting Trappist ale with symbolic value." Originally slated to be sold exclusively in 2009, its popularity earned it a spot in the permanent line-up of La Trappe's family of beers.

La Trappe Tripel (8% ABV)

La Trappe's Tripel blends beautiful Belgian yeast aroma with a light, refreshing finish. It pours a dark honey color in the glass that is slightly hazy from the second addition of yeast.

Brewery at La Trappe. *Caroline Wallace*

Fermentation tanks at the La Trappe brewery. *Caroline Wallace*

33 cL bottles are recycled, cleaned, and filled with La Trappe beer on the bottling line. *Caroline Wallace*

Packaged bottles ready for distribution. *Caroline Wallace*

La Trappe Dubbel for sale in the abbey shop. *Caroline Wallace*

A peek inside the barrel room. *Caroline Wallace*

La Trappe Quadrupel (10% ABV)

This Quadrupel has a heavy, alcohol-forward body and a rich amber color. It is malty, nutty, with soft vanilla notes that tantalize the senses. It ages well in the bottle, so purchase one for now and one for later!

La Trappe Quadrupel Oak Aged (10% ABV)

La Trappe's Quadrupel is aged in oak barrels. The unique, complex flavor depends on the type of vessel and makes this offering rather special. Port, white wine, and whiskey barrels are among the varieties utilized.

La Trappe Bockbier (7% ABV, Seasonal)

This beer is the first Trappist bock and is produced seasonally. Full of rich, caramelly sweet malt and aromatic hops, it pours a deep auburn with a thick beige foam. Dark fruit notes meld with the slightly bitter roasted malt flavor.

TRAVEL TIPS

La Trappe boasts an expansive and manicured tasting room open varying hours seasonally (check the website). Here visitors can try the entire impressive family of La Trappe's brews paired wisely with flavorful dishes. On the menu is also abbey bread and cheese, including cheeses and sauces made from La Trappe beers. With a beautiful view of the grounds visitors may also catch a glimpse of a monk—a welcome and novel sight for any abbey visit.

Solidifying its position as one of the most easily accessible Trappist breweries, La Trappe offers "Excursions"—brewery tours given in English or Dutch and broken down into three packages:

Excursion:

1.5 hours (12 euros)
A tour of the brewery, a movie about life in the monastery and the brewery, and one "consumption of your choice."

Excursion and Beer Tasting:

2.5 hours (19.5 euros)
A tour of the brewery, a movie about life in the monastery and the brewery, one "consumption of your choice," and four La Trappe tasting glasses.

And finally, the pièce de résistance. . .

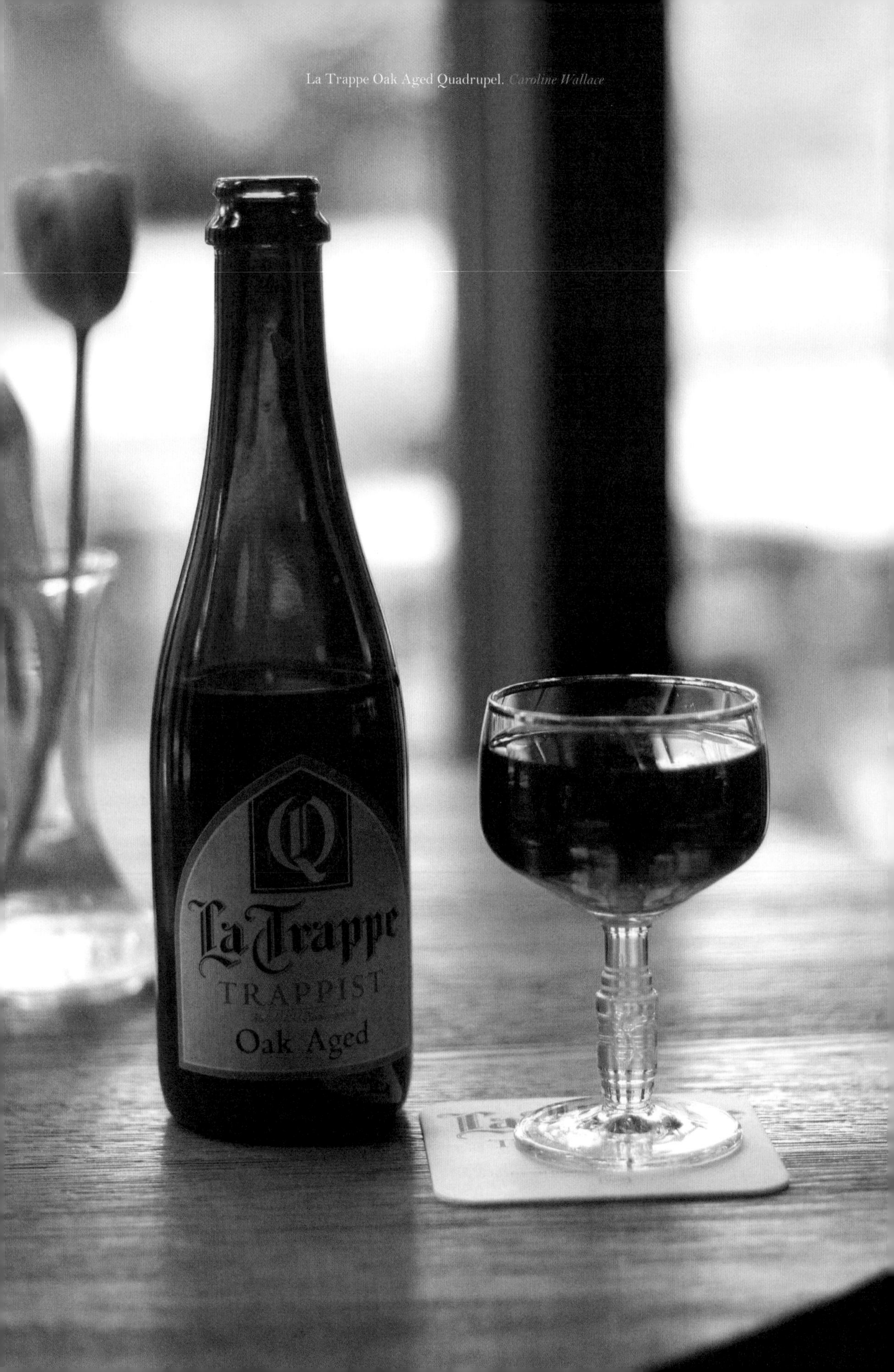

La Trappe Oak Aged Quadrupel. *Caroline Wallace*

**Excursion and Beer Tasting and Snacks:
2.5 hours (29.5 euros)**
A tour of the brewery, a movie about life in the monastery and the brewery, one "consumption of your choice," four La Trappe tasting glasses, and four "traditional snacks." It probably goes without saying, but we vote for splurging on the snacks.

The "Kloosterwinkel," which translates to "monastery shop" in Dutch, is Koningshoeven's abbey gift shop. It is open varying hours seasonally (again, the website's got you covered) and sells all of La Trappe's ales, along with matching commemorative glassware and gift sets, chocolates, beer bread, soap, cheese, jam, and more. The website proclaims, "La Trappe is ale you experience, and should be accompanied by products that can match that experience." Hear hear.

A smattering of biking routes stem from and around the abbey, ranging from 19 to 47 miles long. Once again, the abbey's website provides valuable information. Links to geotagged maps mark each bicycle route, and La Trappe even offers charging stations for electric bikes.

The abbey shop sells an assortment of Trappist wares, including beer. *Caroline Wallace*

Patrons enjoying lunch on the patio outside the tasting room. *Courtesy of Koningshoeven Abbey*

Bike routes around Koningshoeven Abbey are a popular option for visitors to the abbey. *Caroline Wallace*

ROCHEFORT

Abbey Notre-Dame de Saint-Remy (Rochefort Abbey)
Rochefort Brewery
Rochefort, Belgium

Rochefort illustration. *Jessica Deahl*

05. Rochefort

Abbey Notre-Dame de Saint-Remy (Rochefort Abbey)
Rochefort Brewery
Rochefort, Belgium

Situated in the south of Belgium, in the Walloon region near the French border, is the Abbey Notre-Dame de Saint-Remy. It is a stoic and quiet bastion nestled in a thickly forested hill just a few miles from the town of Rochefort. We follow a modest road winding through the forest and up to the abbey, a mysterious oasis tucked away in the trees. Strategically set apart from the distractions of modernity, the monks here spend their days in quiet contemplation, prayer, and manual work. Some of the best beers in the world are made behind these walls.

As we park in a small lot outside the abbey gates. we aren't quite sure how to announce our arrival without accidentally being impolite. When it comes to monks we are well advised to be patient. A quick French-English translation of a handwritten sign on the entrance window informs us visitors are not allowed. Not being a tourist destination, there is no gift shop and casual brewery tours are not granted. This is to protect the solitary nature of monastic life, and Rochefort Abbey is one of the most isolated of the Trappist breweries. Fortunately, we have made special arrangements to stay in the guest quarters for a few nights. The abbey does offer extended visits for those interested in a spiritual retreat, but this is not typical tourism.

We perch on a small wall adjacent to what we assume is the front entrance and wait for something to happen. The scene is lovely—a large red brick porch and tower with a small private garden running alongside. We muse about ringing a bell hanging in front of the entrance. Is that just for special occasions or

Stained glass inside the guest quarters. *Jessica Deahl*

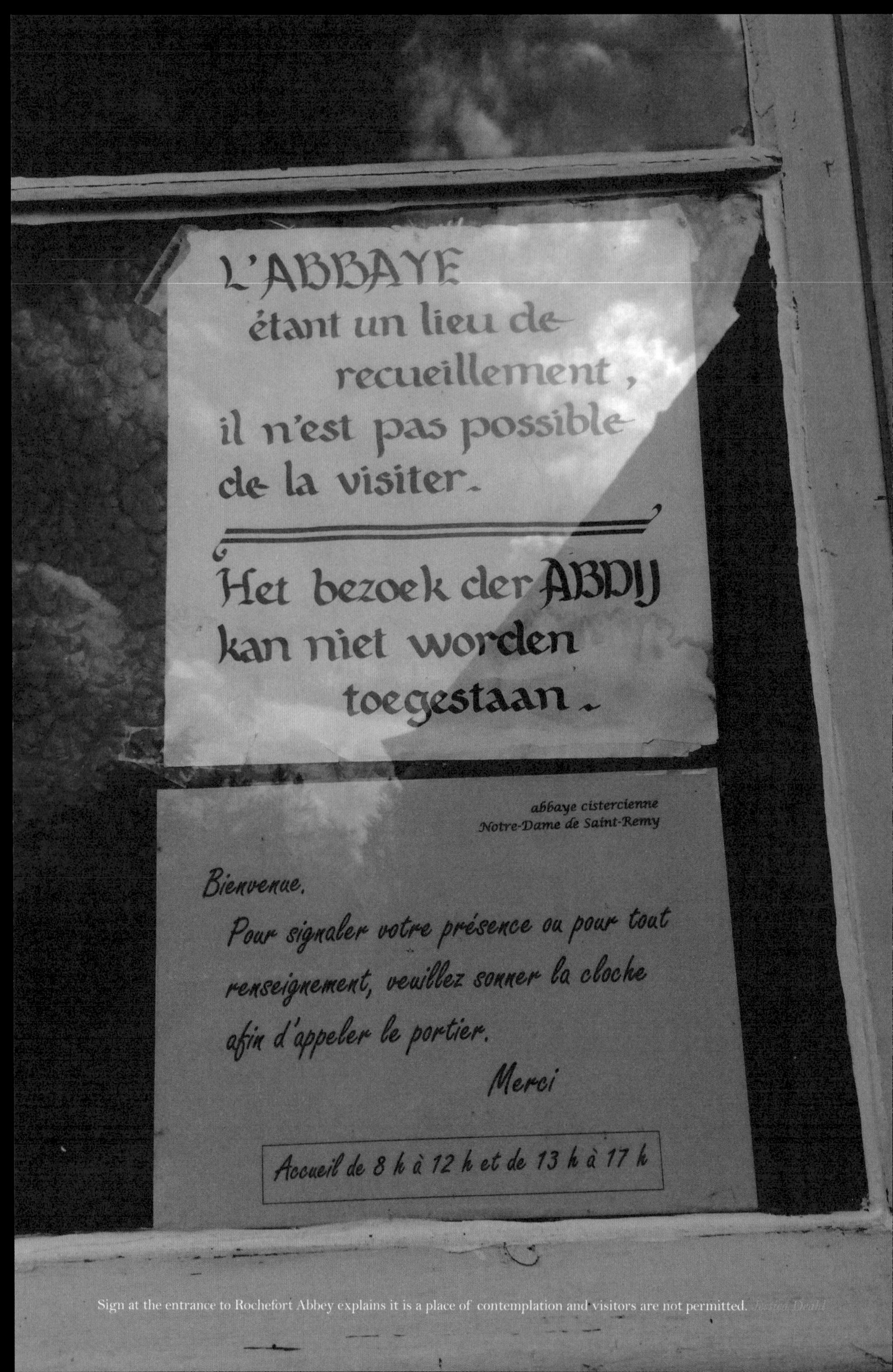

L'ABBAYE
étant un lieu de
recueillement,
il n'est pas possible
de la visiter.

Het bezoek der **ABDIJ**
kan niet worden
toegestaan.

abbaye cistercienne
Notre-Dame de Saint-Remy

Bienvenue.

Pour signaler votre présence ou pour tout

renseignement, veuillez sonner la cloche

afin d'appeler le portier.

Merci

Accueil de 8 h à 12 h et de 13 h à 17 h

Sign at the entrance to Rochefort Abbey explains it is a place of contemplation and visitors are not permitted.

Keys to a guest room. *Jessica Deahl*

religious ceremony? What happens if we just knock? It seems far too quiet to disturb the peace. Our naïvety begs caution, so we wait.

It does not take long before the front door swings wide, revealing a cheerful, vibrant monk named Brother Gregoire, who greets us with open arms. We speak very little French and our monk host speaks very little English, but he could not possibly be more welcoming or charming. He dons the traditional Cistercian garb: a white robe covered by a black hooded scapular and a brown belt. He eagerly shows us our individual rooms for the night, gracious little hideaways on the second floor. We find beds with crisp, clean sheets and writing desks upon which are lists of the weekly and daily prayer schedules and literature about the Catholic Church.

Following a quiet dinner we retire to bed for the evening. Without access to our typical Internet-fueled diets of e-mail, status updates, and Click Hole lists, there is little to distract us. Strategically removing life's unnecessary diversions and interruptions, Trappist monks are able to live a life of purpose and contemplation. At precisely 3:30 the next

morning the bell rings to signal the morning prayer and start of the monks' day. We let ourselves sleep for a few more hours until breakfast but take note of the daily dedication that monastic life requires.

CISTERCIANS AND REFORM: THE HISTORY OF ROCHEFORT ABBEY

The next day we meet with Secrétaire Commercial (Business Secretary) Benoît Minet of the Abbey Notre-Dame de Saint-Remy to discuss the abbey's history, brewery, and future plans. Benoît has a pleasant manner and eagerly engages our questioning. He has been employed at the abbey since 2011, following his role managing the economic development of a nearby municipality. We all sit in the morning sun in the garden beneath our guesthouse windows, acutely aware of the stillness. The only sounds, save for a few chirping birds, are our voices. Accompanied by our French interpreter Océane, we begin our discussion with the history of the abbey.

The abbey at Rochefort is an example of the vast reforms and revivals of the greater

Benoît Minet, business secretary for the abbey. *Caroline Wallace*

Cistercian Order over the centuries and a representation of hope and tenacity for Trappist monks as a whole.

The story of all Trappist abbeys really starts with Cîteaux. With the intention of the literal observance of the Rule of Saint Benedict, a group of Benedictine monks founded an abbey at Cîteaux in 1098 and embraced a "Cistercian" lifestyle. The first Cistercians sought simplicity and worked only to have the basic necessities of life by following the motto of *pax* ("peace") and *ora et labora* ("pray and work"). By the end of the twelfth century, the order had spread throughout France and to greater Europe (*Observantiae*, 31). By 1230, it had reached Belgium and the Secours de Notre-Dame, a group of nuns associated with the Cistercian Order, was established at the site by Gilles de Walcourt (the Count of Rochefort). This community of pious ladies erected a monastery called "Help Our Lady" (*Succursus Dominae Nostrae*). In 1239 Count Henri of Luxembourg gave the nuns a tenth of Hans-Sur-Lesse, a district of the town of Rochefort along the Lesse river. This river

was instrumental in the erosion of limestone that developed the caves at Han known worldwide and a major tourist attraction for the region today.

The peace and tranquility at the abbey reveals very little about its rocky past. During the fourteenth and fifteenth centuries times were pretty rough for the Cistercian Order and Europe in general. Destructive weaknesses of human nature, excessive economic costs of the abbeys, and the ravages of war all took their toll on the health of many Cistercian communities. Religious zeal and discipline among the abbeys deteriorated, and a split in the Roman Catholic Church historically known as the Western Schism (fifteenth century) led to continuing reform of the Order from Cîteaux. A more strict application of the Rule of Saint Benedict was employed, and several women's monasteries were turned over to monks (*Observantiae*, 32).

In 1464 the nuns at Rochefort were ordered to move to the Félipré monastery near Givet, France. Abbots were sent by the General Chapter of the Cistercian Order to report on the plight of the abbey, and they found it had become heavily indebted, its buildings dilapidated and in disrepair. Lord of Rochefort Louis de la Marck endorsed this unique swap of nuns and monks, so the Félipré monks took over Rochefort Abbey. Thus began a new and short-lived period of prosperity for the abbey. Now under direct control of Cîteaux, the Cistercian monks at Rochefort were able to better exploit the resources of the area and the abbey thrived.

Things took a problematic turn for Rochefort again in the sixteenth and seventeenth centuries. During the Eighty Years War (Dutch War of Independence), the abbey was devastated by the Protestant armies of the Seventeen Provinces (1568) and the Austrian armies of John of Austria (1577). Shortly after, the Trappist monks at Rochefort decided to start brewing for the first time; an accounting document traces beer production at the monastery to 1595. A lack of potable water and the viability of cereal grains in the area encouraged the making of beer at the abbey. Beer production remained rather small and would be

Inside the abbey walls. *Caroline Wallace*

In the garden at Rochefort Abbey. *Caroline Wallace*

The abbey's motto *Curvato resurgo* ("Bent, I stand up again") engraved on the walls of the abbey farm. *Caroline Wallace*

Beautiful architectural details adorn the facade. *Caroline Wallace*

consumed primarily on the premises for the next few hundred years.

Turmoil during the seventeenth century, including a string of wars, looting, occupations, and arson, took its toll on the region. In 1650 French troops looted and occupied the abbey, leaving it in shambles the following year. Reconstruction work began in 1664, and a new church was consecrated in 1671. Abbot Phillipe Fabry (1654–1684)

engraved his motto *Curvata resurgo* ("Bent, I stand up again") under his coat of arms, and the monastery has embraced it ever since. The coat of arms depicts a star representing faith, a palm tree for hope, and a rose for charity. It can be seen today on the walls of the abbey farm.

Disaster befell again in 1789, when revolutionists stormed the Bastille in Paris and the French Revolution began. The abbey was again occupied by soldiers, and beer production halted. Influenced by the ideas of the revolutionists, the abbey of Rochefort requested to be secularized. It was then closed and sold in 1797 to layman Lucien-Joseph Poncelet, who demolished the abbey and converted it to a farm in 1805.

Nearly a century later in 1889, monastic life was restored at the Rochefort abbey. In 1887 Father Anselmus Judong traveled from the abbey at Achel, and his monks took over the remaining buildings and began to restore the site. Now a "daughter house" of Achel, the monks decided to support this new period of growth with the installation of a new brewing program. Today Achel (and, by proxy, Rochefort) are dependent on Westmalle Abbey.

Due to centuries of destruction and reconstruction, almost none of the abbey's architecture is original; the collection of

Monastic life was restored at the abbey in 1889. *Caroline Wallace*

buildings represents no cohesive style. "We just try to keep a global harmony between them," Minet mentions. The oldest buildings are the farm and the porch, from the fifteenth and sixteenth centuries, respectively.

Rochefort is well known for its marble, and exploitation of the quarry from the sixteenth to the twentieth century (which was closed permanently in 1970) yielded rose and white marble that was used in Saint Peter's Basilica and the Versailles castle. The abbey church is reminiscent of a Roman style, constructed in 1900 and renovated in 1990 using stones from France. It is in this sober, impressive space that the thirteen monks living at the abbey meet daily to pray and chant hymns. On the floor of the church is a large tile labyrinth modeled after one in the "Our Lady" cathedral in Chartres. Things at the abbey have remained relatively stable in recent years, save for a fire that broke out in 2010. Fortunately no one was injured and the vessels of Rochefort beer were spared.

After a tour of the abbey grounds Benoît invites us to participate in an afternoon service in the church. Though the monks

Interior of the church at Rochefort Abbey, where the monks meet for daily mass, is also open to visitors. *Luca Galuzzi (www.galuzzi.it)*

spend much of their day in spaces separate from the public, they welcome the local community to take part in daily mass. Only a few rows of pews accommodate this, and today we are joined by just one other gentleman. Benoît points out that (as we are familiar with in American tradition) the church sees many more visitors on holidays and special occasions. We admire the simplicity of the inner architecture as a handful of monks file silently into the sanctuary, ever-smiling Brother Gregoire among their ranks. What follows is a short ceremony of Gregorian songs in French and Latin. After a few hymns Gregoire rings a bell and the function is complete. The monks retreat through the back of the church to resume their activities in the cloister as quietly and mysteriously as they entered.

HISTORY OF BREWING AT ROCHEFORT

Until the 1950s, brewing at Rochefort remained a small activity behind farming, animal husbandry, beekeeping, the marble quarry, and forest exploration. Little by little, the monks abandoned the farm and developed the brewery. Economic changes demanded a shift in monastic work from the land, and Rochefort officially gave up agricultural endeavors in 1983. Benoît points out that traditionally Cistercian monks (and specifically Trappists) "hold manual work in high esteem, particularly working with soil." Ever resilient, Rochefort Abbey adapted to changing times and revived its brewing program.

To do this, they looked to Scourmont Abbey in Chimay, which had implemented a successful Trappist brewery. Scourmont's Father Abbot Theodore and Professor Jean De Clerck from the University of Leuven helped Rochefort improve its brewing activities on all levels. The University of Leuven had worked closely with the Chimay monks to

isolate a yeast strain and to train Father Theodore to become a master brewer. The collaboration proved fruitful for Chimay, and the brewery was soon busily producing their popular Premiére and Grande Réserve.

This partnership was also incredibly useful for Rochefort. A young Father Hubert, who would eventually become Father Abbot of Rochefort, was sent to Chimay to learn to brew. The recipe and quality of beer was improved as new equipment was installed. The yeast strain unique to Rochefort beers was selected and propagated on the abbey's grounds. A protected strain of this yeast is

Bottle distribution in the early days. *Courtesy of Rochefort Abbey*

Monks brewing. *Courtesy of Rochefort Abbey*

kept for safety at the University of Leuven. Rochefort's beer portfolio is based on these recipes established and developed during the 1950s, and today the beers are revered by many as some of the best examples of Belgian or Belgian-style beer worldwide.

THE CATHEDRAL OF BEER

The brewery today is as humbling as it is state of the art. If Trappists do anything, they do it the right way—with a special finesse and attention to detail—and that has solidified their role as world class brewers. Tall, thin, stained glass windows extend from floor to ceiling, and the warm light bounces off the brewery's Meura copper kettles. Dubbed the "cathedral of beer," this brewhouse feels just as much like a place of worship as the church itself. It is here the Rochefort Trappist Ales (Trappistes Rochefort) are produced. Rochefort is known and respected for its robust brown ales that include only natural products: spring water, malted barley, hops, sugar, and a proprietary yeast strain. The simply named Rochefort 6, 8, and 10 get their classification from an ancient measure of density that hints at each beer's alcohol content.

"Rochefort's role is to maintain a high brand image of the Trappist breweries over the world," Minet says.

They focus on three main points: quality of beer, history, and originality of product. A prerequisite of Trappist life is producing goods to support the community. Monks value manual work, and this approach is apparent in the quality of ingredients and the special attention given to the brewing process.

He explains that Rochefort's beer is a "beer of tradition. . .it is important to us that people who like Rochefort understand the story that led the monks in our country to make beers."

As with all Trappist beers bearing the Authentic Trappist Product mark, it must be brewed on premises, overseen by the monks, and yield enough revenue to support the needs of the monastery. Production is necessarily limited, and is currently at 45,000 hL (approximately 38,000 barrels) a year. Any excess profit generated is redistributed in a way that the community agrees is appropriate, including funding to sustain other Trappist monasteries, helping families near Rochefort that are in financial need, and donations to a variety of charitable organizations and associations in the region.

It is of utmost importance to the abbey that they produce an original and distinguishable beer that is immediately recognizable by consumers. This begins with water—and Rochefort's famously comes from the Tridaine stream. The abbey has gone to great lengths to ensure the stream water remains pure and not chemically treated. The stream water remains a point of pride for Rochefort and arguably contributes a distinctive taste and specialness to its lineup of beers.

Of the thirteen monks at Rochefort abbey, three are involved in the brewing process in an administrative capacity, overseeing accounting, human resources, business meetings, and handling quality control, all with the goal of ensuring a world class family of beers bearing the Trappist mark. The other monks at the abbey have different responsibilities at the monastery depending on their age or capacity. To keep production rolling sixteen laypersons are currently employed to brew and package the beers.

The abbey sells its 33 cL bottles directly to wholesalers and supermarket chains in Belgium, as well as to large export markets in Europe and beyond. The beers are also exported through some Belgian wholesalers, and the entire roster can be purchased in the United States. Rochefort Trappist beers are available to consume at many cafés near Rochefort abbey but are never served on tap. They are best served at a temperature around 54°F in the original Trappistes Rochefort balloon glass.

The spectacular Rochefort brewhouse. *Caroline Wallace*

A selection of historical artifacts is on display beneath the brewhouse. *Jessica Deahl*

Light bounces off copper kettles in the "Cathedral of Beer." *Jessica Deahl*

A small reminder on the brewhouse wall. *Caroline Wallace*

Calibrating the centrifuge. *Jessica Deahl*

Water for Rochefort beer is sourced from nearby Tridaine stream. *Jessica Deahl*

The Rochefort brewhouse. *Caroline Wallace*

The bottling line at Rochefort brewery. *Jessica Deahl*

THE BEER

Rochefort 6 (7.5% ABV)

Rochefort's Dubbel, topped with a red cap, is a delicate and sophisticated brew. The oldest of Rochefort's lineup, its origins can be traced to the abbey brewery's first beer recipe. This was the only beer brewed until World War II. The modern iteration of Rochefort 6 was developed during the abbey's collaboration with Chimay and was introduced to the market in 1953.

This Dubbel pours a hazy, light amber brown. It is malt-forward, with a touch of sweetness and a hint of sour. Rochefort 6 is perhaps the least complex of the Rochefort family; it is simply a delicious beer. It pairs well with a modest refectory dinner.

Rochefort 8 (9.2% ABV)

Rochefort 8 is the brewery's strong dark ale. It originated as a seasonal beer brewed only for New Year's Eve celebrations. The beer's overwhelming popularity encouraged the monks to include it in the regular lineup in the early 1960s.

Distinctive by its green cap, Rochefort 8 is certainly special. While all of Rochefort's beers use a variation on the same recipe, the amount of candy sugar and malt used in the brewing makes each distinct. Rochefort 8 pours a deep brown color, highly carbonated and full of body. The aroma is of chocolate and dark fruit. The rich, sweet taste strikes a perfect balance with an alcohol content that is not to be scoffed at.

Rochefort 10 (11.3% ABV)

Rounding out the series, this Quadrupel is big and bold. Bearing the blue cap, Rochefort 10 utilizes pils and caramel malts and a hefty dose of candy sugar. Not for the faint of heart, this Quadrupel demands attention and contemplation, qualities reminiscent of monastic life.

A monk checks in on the bottling line. *Caroline Wallace*

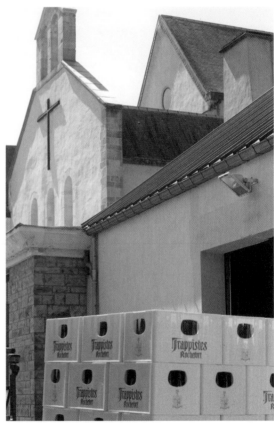
Outside the Rochefort brewery. *Caroline Wallace*

A welcome contribution to the table for its nutrient content, Rochefort 10 certainly reinforces the common colloquialism describing beer as "liquid bread." It pours almost like chocolate milk. Rich with sediment, it reminds the consumer that all of the Rochefort beers are bottle-conditioned with extra yeast and sugar. Dark fruit, alcohol, and yeast are layered with caramelly sweetness. As it warms, the taste evolves and delights. This beer is to be sipped and savored.

TRAVEL TIPS

The region and land surrounding the abbey is fruitful and bountiful. The Tridaine stream flows from a water table near Rochefort, providing pure, unfiltered water for the beer as well as acting as a gratis source of water for the city. The area is well known for its many caves (grottos) and a nearby rose and white marble quarry. Tourists in and around Rochefort enjoy visiting the caves in Han-Sur-Lesse and the nearby wild animal park; the meandering roads throughout the surrounding hills are also a popular destination for hikers and cyclists.

The abbey does not have an operating gift shop or café, but Rochefort beers can be enjoyed at many restaurants and taverns in the nearby village of the same name. There are accommodations at the abbey in guesthouses for those seeking spiritual retreat and contemplation.

AREA ATTRACTIONS

Take the Han-Sur-Lesse cave tour. Do not let the childlike illustration of a cave dweller on the sign deter you; it may look like it is only valuable for Belgian children on a field trip, but trust us. A generous (and bilingual) tour of centuries-old stalactites and stalagmites awaits. There is also a bonus light show orchestrated to Enya-esque music that is uplifting and bewildering.

Rochefort 8 bottle and glass. *Caroline Wallace*

Rochefort beers in the signature balloon glass. *Caroline Wallace*

CHIMAY

Abbaye Notre-Dame de Scourmont (Scourmont Abbey)
Bieres du Chimay
Chimay, Belgium

Chimay illustration. *Jessica Deahl*

06. Chimay

Abbaye Notre-Dame de Scourmont (Scourmont Abbey)
Bieres du Chimay
Chimay, Belgium

During our planning process we braced ourselves for the experience at Scourmont Abbey, home of the largest of the Trappist breweries, Chimay. Like many American beer lovers, Chimay was one of our first introductions to Belgian style beer, and it has become mildly paradoxical as we have gone deeper in our research of the Trappist way of life. Chimay is widely available globally. Its production capacity dwarfs any other Trappist brewery's annual production multiple times. It is a behemoth brewery in any meter of measure. The mechanism at work that allows all of this to live harmoniously within the walls of a quiet, secluded Trappist monastery is as great a mystery to us as the monks that oversee the work.

With all of this contemplation at play internally, our drive from Rochefort through the Hainaut province of Belgium has a near-electric charge to it. We talk excitedly about what our interview will hold. Representatives of Chimay provided us with a full agenda of our tour prior to our trip, ranging from a tour of the cheese factory to an aerial view of the idyllic countryside by plane. We are anxious to see how all this will flavor the story of the monks and beer that is being produced within their community.

The day is warm and this region of Belgium is like the setting of a fairy tale. We drive through gentle rolling hills along well-forested and shaded roads and see ancient cities going about their business on a Thursday morning.

The town of Chimay is nestled in the Walloon, the French-speaking portion of Belgium. It has a population of around 10,000.

The recognizable Chimay seal posted prominently outside the brewery's cellar. *Caroline Wallace*

When the community expanded their brewery, they donated the old copper brew kettles to the town of Chimay as a gift. One now resides in one of the town's most heavily trafficked roundabouts. *Caroline Wallace*

As we enter the town we see a copper brew kettle sitting ornamentally in the middle of a roundabout, a gift from the abbey signifying the deep connection between the two entities. It is unexpected but incredibly charming as we familiarize ourselves with the area.

As we near the Bieres de Chimay offices we note how industrial the area is. Clearly this is not the location of Scourmont Abbey, but an off-site location to minimize the amount of churn and bustle the Brothers of Scourmont need to entertain on a daily basis.

Tap handles in one of the brewery's formal tasting rooms. *Caroline Wallace*

While the beer is still brewed at Scourmont Abbey, therefore conforming to International Trappist Association stipulations for Authentic Trappist Product (ATP) qualification, it is shuttled off site for bottling after the brew is fermented.

We walk into the reception area and are greeted kindly by a young woman. She tells us Fabrice Bordon will be joining us shortly. We take a seat and watch as employees come in and out, greeting each other with a friendly hello or a warm kiss on the cheek. There is an established culture of goodwill and community here, not unlike what we have seen at the communities we have already visited.

Fabrice shakes our hands heartily. He is the epitome of European charm: professionally dressed and polite and congenial, with very kind features. From the way he speaks, it is clear to us he has a deep love for Scourmont and Chimay. He excitedly takes us on our way, breaking into the history of the monastery and the incredible journey it has taken establishing Bieres de Chimay.

Fabrice Bordon, sales manager of exports. *Caroline Wallace*

Scourmont Abbey from above. *Caroline Wallace*

FORGING SCOURMONT ABBEY

Scourmont Abbey has been inhabited by Trappist brothers since 1850. Conversations began in 1844, when Father Jean-Baptiste Jourdain, a local Belgian priest, began sourcing support from the Prince of Chimay Joseph II de Chimay to establish a Trappist community in the area. The prince granted Jourdain permission to build on a plateau in his kingdom called Scourmont. All attempts to cultivate the property had proven futile prior to the monks' arrival, but in July 1850, a group of around twenty monks arrived from Scourmont's mother abbey (Saint-Sixtus) to build a priory.

The land proved to be as unyielding as its history implied; over 100,000 tons of rock was excised from the soil for crops and cattle to take to the new pasture.

The land did have one gift to offer: a natural and dedicated source of water from a nearby well. This well now feeds the brewery all the water necessary to make Chimay's beers. Its distinct waters impart a particular flavor to the beer that the community holds very dear.

The guesthouses and welcome center of Scourmont Abbey.
Caroline Wallace

Despite initial hardship, after twelve short years the brothers had established a life for themselves. They had built a priory, a farm for crops, and a dairy to produce butter. They next wanted to move toward a self-sustainable source for their beer. They began brewing in 1862 to meet this goal. This early recipe was not the traditional Belgian-style beer Trappists are known for today, nor was it the iconic red, blue, or white capped bottles Chimay produces today, but a simpler Bock-style brew.

The gardens in the courtyard at Scourmont.

Inside the church of Scourmont Abbey.

While this Bock certainly served its purpose, the community was still in contact with its mother abbey. Brothers at Westvleteren were brewing a dark beer the Community at Scourmont desired to learn and experiment with. Eventually these experimentations evolved into Chimay Première, better known today as Chimay Rouge. It was Chimay Première that was first made available to the public for purchase in 750 ml bottles to aid in sustaining life at Scourmont Abbey.

FROMAGE DE CHIMAY

In 1876 the brothers began utilizing their dairy cows to make cheese to sustain their monastic way of life.

Cheese at Chimay is closely tied to the brewery and the flavors of beer produced within the monastery's walls. Behind the main offices, next to the bottling facilities, there is a large warehouse that contains the dairy, processing acres of cow's milk cheese each

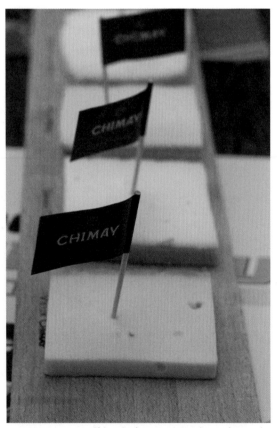

Chimay's cheese program is as robust as its beer offerings, utilizing the beer in many of the cheeses produced. *Caroline Wallace*

day made to the exact specifications of the monks' more than 100 years of tradition.

The milk is sourced from farms within eighteen miles of the dairy. It is stored and analyzed in the dairy's lab to ensure safety, since the milk arrives unpasteurized. Then Chimay's fromagers begin the process of making cheese.

The milk is blended, curdled, molded, and pressed into various shapes and sizes of finished wheels of cheese. It is here the different varieties begin to form their distinctions.

There are seven varieties of cheese produced at the Chimay dairy, each one touting specific characteristics that make it the perfect beer mate to each one of the four Chimay beers.

There is Chimay cheese à la Chimay Grande Reserve that is aged in the dairy's cheese cellars for two weeks and washed in Chimay Blue.

There is cheese à la Chimay Première, which is pressed into larger, 2 kg wheels, aged for three weeks, and washed in Chimay Rouge.

Also produced are the Poteaupré, the Dore cheese, Grand Chimay, Chimay Grand Cru, and Vieux Chimay. While these cheeses are not washed in beer like the cheese à la Grande Reserve and cheese à la Première, they age between three weeks and twelve months to provide a vast range in flavor and texture across the dairy's portfolio.

CARVING A NEW START

As with many European Trappist abbeys, World War II deeply reshaped the history of this community. During the four-year German occupation, the monastery's walls were controlled and inhabited by German troops. The monks fled or were called up for service. The community of more than sixty monks was displaced for the entirety of the war. Those who attempted to stay or aid were persecuted by the Germans, and when they returned in 1944, they found their home in ruins. Much of the monastery had been destroyed and needed rebuilding. The brewing equipment had been stripped down and repurposed for the war effort. Scourmont was almost unrecognizable.

The courtyard outside of the guesthouses and monks' living quarters. *Jessica Deahl*

Instead of succumbing to this loss, the brothers capitalized on the opportunity to start anew. They rebuilt the monastery and the brewery, but were out of practice brewing, and the beer suffered. It was decided a young monk named Brother Theodore would travel to the University Leuven to study the craft of brewing under renowned beer scientist Jean De Clerck.

De Clerck, touted by many to be the most influential scientific voice of the twentieth century in the brewing industry, wrote the

Father Theodore's original pilot brew system with an image of the well-known brother at work. *Caroline Wallace*

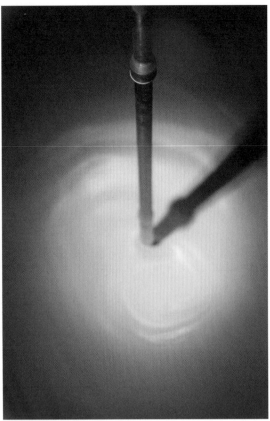

The brewing of a Chimay beer. *Caroline Wallace*

book aptly named *A Textbook of Brewing*, which multitudes have used as the definitive standard on brewing since it was published in 1948. Brother Theodore, who was destined for the role of abbot and title Father, was in excellent hands and built a very strong relationship with De Clerck during his education at Leuven.

More prolific than their friendship was the output of Father Theodore's and De Clerck's work together: a proprietary strain of yeast that would set the flavor of Chimay's beers apart from any other in the world. For two years Father Theodore worked in the laboratory he established in the brewery, isolating a strain of yeast that would be most complementary to the flavor profile he envisioned for the beers. In 1948 the community began selling Chimay Première with the new yeast. That strain is still carefully propagated and used in all of Chimay's beers. The year 1948 is also when Chimay released Première in 330 mL bottles, as well as the traditional 750 ml.

Throughout the next few decades, Father Theodore revolutionized the Chimay beer

The branding of Chimay beer has gone through many iterations since the 1950s. *Caroline Wallace*

A display illustrating the evolution of Chimay's packaging over the years. *Caroline Wallace*

program at Scourmont Abbey. He was constantly trying out pilot batches in his miniature brewhouse, tweaking recipes here and there to enhance nuances that might otherwise have been lost.

Shortly after the release of bottles of Chimay Rouge with proprietary yeast, Father Theodore brewed a special Christmas ale called Spéciale Noël. At 9.0% ABV the dark garnet beer was not to be taken lightly. With notes of dried dark fruits, chocolate, and yeast, it was an instant hit. The beer was so successful that during Christmas 1954, Chimay began producing it year-round. Today it is known as Chimay Grande Réserve or Chimay Bleue.

In 1986 for the town of Chimay's five-hundredth anniversary, the Community at Scourmont Abbey released a special celebratory beer that had a character reminiscent of champagne called Chimay Cinq Cents, or more commonly today Chimay Blanche.

This beer was a special investment of Father Theodore's time and energy. He had a deep love for beers that were a little more hop-forward. He had created a recipe very similar to that of the Blanche twenty years prior to its release, but made it in such small batches bottling was never a viable option. It took a momentous occasion to coax out the hoppy Tripel from the abbey's walls.

Chimay's popularity really exploded internationally during the last thirty years of the twentieth century, when European "Special Beer" (craft beer) popularity was on the rise globally. In Belgium and surrounding countries beer had always held a very important place culturally at the table. People were starting to realize this outside these countries' borders. Chimay was especially well placed to international renown due to the strict quality standards Trappists demand from their products. The beer was exceptional, and as more and more people tasted it, they wanted it stocked on shelves back home.

BREWING BIG THE TRAPPIST WAY

Chimay is sold in tens of dozens of countries around the globe, giving reason to the millions of gallons of beer being produced annually.

A detail in the Chimay Experience. *Caroline Wallace*

Currently Chimay produces four beers: Chimay Première (Chimay Rouge), Chimay Grande Réserve (Chimay Bleue), Chimay Cinq Cents (Chimay Blanche), and their newest public offering Chimay Doree, a patersbier previously reserved for brothers, visitors to the abbey, and guests at the nearby affiliated Inn Poteaupré. The newest Chimay beer goes by the colloquial name Chimay Gold.

While sixteen brothers still live and work at Scourmont, the technical production and handling of beer is done by laypeople. Father Abbott oversees the production and participates in tastings during the final stages of beer production, but outside of that the community relies on outside help to keep the giant Chimay production schedule on track.

Production on these four beers is booming, albeit a quiet boom in the brewery behind the church at Scourmont Abbey. The community produces over twelve megaliters of beer annually—over 75,000 barrels, or nearly 3.5 million gallons of beer per year.

Chimay houses a chemical and microbiological lab in their brewing facility, so there is no shortage of measurable data being captured by the layman brewers. Each

Chimay's brew kettles today will produce more beer annually than many other breweries combined. *Caroline Wallace*

Hot wort is filtered through this cooling system to bring it to a temperature appropriate for yeast to live. *Caroline Wallace*

step of the brewing process calls for specific tests to ensure the beer is developing characteristics consistent with the quality of Chimay's output over the last seventy years. From checking the gravity of wort to verifying the vitality of a collection of yeast, there is no test too menial for the labs.

There is also a fully automated, state-of-the-art brewhouse mashing malt into wort and boiling hops for Chimay's portfolio. The tons of spent grain generated are sent to local dairy farmers to sustain their cattle. We could not help but notice the cows in the region, apart from being incredibly well fed, were also very content looking specimens.

After the brewing process, the beer is clarified via centrifuge and fills one of Chimay's fermenters. These stainless steel towers are each five stories tall and are accessed by a series of ramps and platforms.

The brewers of Chimay also have a unique yeast propagation tank on the ground floor of the fermentation room to keep their proprietary strain clean and healthy.

Today brewers at Chimay are also experimenting with barrel aging in White Oak for a very limited release of Grande Reserve. In the very bottom floor of the brewery there is a row of pristine white barrels embellished with a Chimay brand sitting in wait to unleash a Chimay unlike any the world has tasted.

After several weeks in active fermentation the beer is moved into lagering tanks to finish the beer making process. It is then loaded into refrigerated trucks and taken back to the main offices away from the abbey for bottling. During this step the last addition of yeast and sugar are added to the beer as it is pumped into the trucks.

Down the road at the bottling plant, used bottles are continually being taken back in, sorted, washed, and sanitized. Bottles from other breweries are removed and shipped to their respective processing centers, while bottles marked with the Scourmont name are refilled with freshly brewed beer.

After a few weeks in storage for the beer's second bottle fermentation, samples of each batch are brought back to the abbey for a final round of tests in the lab and a taste test by a panel of beer experts and Chimay

A member of Chimay's talented brew staff checks levels on one of the brewery's fermenters. *Caroline Wallace*

Bottles of Chimay Bleue age in the Chimay cellar for decades. *Caroline Wallace*

One of Chimay's newest additions to the beer program: barrel aging. *Jessica Deahl*

professionals. If the flavor, color, and aroma are correct for the style, the beer makes its way to shelves around the world.

Chimay retains four bottles of each size produced of every batch of beer, as well as one keg from every batch for the duration of the beer's "best by" window. For Chimay Grande Reserve this window can span decades, and Chimay has established an incredible cellar filled with fifteen, twenty, and even twenty-five-year-old bottles of Chimay Bleue.

As we tour the brewery, Fabrice kindly opens a bottle of Chimay Bleue bottled in 1997. For being old enough to legally vote, the beer is incredibly flavorful, and the cellar is impressive and beautiful.

With its large production size and international distribution map, the beer production at Scourmont Abbey has the potential to do much good financially for other institutes and charities. Chimay funds several sister abbeys in times of financial crisis.

Most noteworthy is Chimay's impact on the township of Chimay overall. Scourmont employs over 30% of the town at the abbey, dairy, bottling plant, and local inn. It also funds multiple local entrepreneurial industries in the Chimay region.

THE BEER

Chimay Dorée (4.80% ABV)

Chimay Doree was once the beer held for the brothers, visitors at the abbey, and patrons at the Auberge du Poteaupré Inn, but was made available globally in 330 mL bottles in 2015. It pours a straw color, with lots of yeast and lemon on the nose. At 4.80% it is the lightest of the Chimay offerings and is very clean with notes of yeast, a touch of spice, a notable hop presence, and a crisp finish.

Chimay Première/Chimay Rouge (7.00% ABV)

The first of Father Theodore's beers to hit the market, Chimay Première is a Dubbel style ale with rich dark fruit notes and a dry finish. It pours a classic medium brown with ruby highlights. It has a chocolate note and a subtle tobacco flavor, but most widely regarded among beer drinkers is the intense dried fruit flavor and creamy finish. At 7.00% ABV it is not to be trifled with, but is not as alcoholic as the Chimay Blanc or Chimay Bleue.

Mr. Fabrice Bordon expertly pours a chalice of Chimay Bleue. *Caroline Wallace*

Scourmont's welcome area houses many resources for guests participating in retreats, but the brewery is not open for visitation to maintain the serenity at the abbey. *Jessica Deahl*

Chimay Cinq Cents/Chimay Blanche
(8.00% ABV)

In 1986, for the town of Chimay's five-hundredth anniversary, the Community at Scourmont Abbey released a special celebratory beer that had a character reminiscent of Champagne. This was called Chimay Cinq Cents, or more commonly today Chimay Blanche. It is considered a hoppy Tripel style ale with a balance between the hop presence and an esthery, peppery aroma. This mid to heavy bodied beer weighs in at a formidable 8.00% ABV.

Chimay Grande Réserve/Chimay Bleue
(9.00% ABV)

Shortly after the release of bottles of Chimay Rouge with proprietary yeast Father Theodore brewed a special Christmas ale called Spéciale Noël. At 9.0% alcohol by volume the dark garnet beer should not be taken lightly. With notes of dried dark fruits, chocolate, and yeast, it was an instant hit. The beer was so successful that in Christmas 1954 Chimay began producing it year-round. Today it is known as Chimay Grande Réserve or Chimay Bleue.

TRAVEL TIPS

While the brewery is not available for tours, visitors to Scourmont are free to walk the property, view the incredible chapel, and tour the abbey cemetery and the well. The brothers welcome those in search of religious retreats and have been known to graciously allow college students a quiet room for intense study sessions around finals time.

Additionally, only a three-minute drive from the abbey's gate is the Poteaupré Inn, where visitors can taste all the Chimay ales paired perfectly with the full line of Chimay cheeses at the inn's restaurant and bar, or choose to spend the night in the accommodations upstairs. The rooms come equipped with a minibar stocked with very reasonably priced Chimay beers.

Downstairs, off the side of the restaurant, there is a museum dedicated to the legacy of the brothers of Scourmont Abbey called the Chimay Experience. It focuses on the beer program and cheese factory and has a full gift shop stocked with any wares Chimay lovers might want, including chalices, clothing, and books.

The Chimay Experience inside the Poteaupré Inn offers an immersive history of Chimay beer steps away from the inn's restaurant, where all the beers are served. *Caroline Wallace*

A chalice of Chimay Blanche outside the Poteaupré Inn. *Caroline Wallace*

WESTVLETEREN

Sint-Sixtusabdij (Saint-Sixtus Abbey)
Westvleteren Brewery
Vleteren, Belgium

Illustration of Saint-Sixtus Abbey. *Jessica Deahl*

07. Westvleteren

Sint-Sixtusabdij (Saint-Sixtus Abbey)
Westvleteren Brewery
Vleteren, Belgium

As we drive the country lane through pastoral West Flanders, passing modest homes and small plots of land with solitary grazing horses, it is hard to fathom that we are en route to the world famous Westvleteren Brewery at Saint-Sixtus Abbey. Upon first sight from the road the abbey feels sleepy and a bit covert, but we realize we are in the right place just in time to glide into the expansive, barren parking lot shared by the abbey and In de Vrede café. It only feels quiet because it is shortly before 10 a.m. (not quite drinkin' hours), but soon this area will be alive with beer pilgrims, locals, and thirsty cyclists looking for a break from all that pedaling. The lone car in the lot belongs to our interpreter Phil, who we are starting to realize is just a compulsively early kind of guy. No qualms with that, Phil.

When we enter the reception area of the abbey we are soon greeted by the cheerful smile of Brother Godfried, who heads up public relations for Saint-Sixtus and its brewery. Brother Godfried greets us warmly in English and tells us he has Googled us in

Stained glass adorns many of the windows at Saint-Sixtus.
Caroline Wallace

Saint-Sixtus Abbey. *Caroline Wallace*

advance of the visit. We take an irrational level of amusement from hearing these words come out of his mouth, and after composing ourselves a bit Brother Godfried leads us through the corridors and begins telling us about the abbey's pre-Google history. His English is fluent, so at this point Phil—a lover of Trappist beer we met in a *BeerAdvocate* forum—is mostly along for the ride to dispense his own pearls of Trappist wisdom and translate the occasional brain buster.

FROM HERMITAGE TO MODERN ABBEY

The land Saint-Sixtus Abbey sits on has been home to monastic communities since as early as 1260, but its Cistercian roots go back to the nineteenth century, when Johannes Baptist Victoor (or Jan-Baptist Victoor) retreated to this land to live as a hermit. In 1831 three monks from the newly formed Trappist monastery Mont-des-Cats in Northern France arrived to join him in his hermitage and a new community was born. Saint-Sixtus grew steadily in numbers, and many years of construction were needed to build the monastery, a brewery, and later an impressive farm.

In 1871, with much of this work now complete, the monastery was elevated to the status of abbey. By 1875, the community had grown to fifty-two monks, even after sending brothers away twice: first to start the daughter house Scourmont Abbey (Chimay) and then to Petit Clairvaux in Nova Scotia (whose community eventually moved to Massachusetts to found Saint Joseph's Abbey, now home to Spencer Brewery). By contrast, today the abbey has just under twenty monks.

Like nearly all of the Trappist abbeys we visit, Saint-Sixtus's history is checkered by the effects of war. During WWI, tens of thousands of Allied soldiers, the majority British and French, were housed at and around the monastery as they clashed with German troops in bloody battles at nearby Ypres. Hundreds of refugees also found protection at the abbey during the war, including a number of orphaned children who slept in the attic of the brewery. Refugees were fed a diet of soup, bread, potatoes, carrots, peas, and beer. While combat never came to the abbey, at least one English soldier—an alleged deserter—was shot on

Saint-Sixtus's community cemetery. *Caroline Wallace*

the abbey grounds by his own command. Today bullet holes still riddle one of the abbey's walls, an ever-present reminder of this dark period.

After the pain and dust of World War I and subsequent World War II started to settle at the abbey, Abbot Dom Gerardus Deleye, who led the community from 1941 to 1968, had to make some key decisions about Saint-Sixtus's future. In 1964 a guesthouse was constructed so groups of visitors seeking spiritual guidance and reflection could visit the abbey for overnight stays. In his last year as abbot Deleye oversaw the construction of a new abbey church that would serve as a prime example of Trappist austerity.

The next period of construction for the abbey took place from 2008 to 2011, when it was discovered the cloister building, which includes the monks' residential quarters, along with the guesthouse, was no longer architecturally sound. Under the direction of Belgian architect Bob Van Reeth a portion of the abbey was demolished and a new cloister was erected. The new building, whose facade we marvel at while we tour the grounds with

Brother Godfried, is a remarkable architectural embodiment of the principle of simplicity the Trappists hold so near and dear. It is also quite modern, which is important to Brother Godfried. He believes that while the brothers should value their rich history, they must also adapt and remain relevant, rather than fading into the past. He believes it is the only way the Order will continue.

One of the most unforgettable physical elements of Saint-Sixtus is its cemetery, where former members of the community have been laid to rest. The peaceful plots sit just outside the church's sturdy doors, a reminder for all the monks who pass by that they are making a commitment to the abbey for life. Each brother's headstone has been cut from the same mother stone, and Brother Godfried explains to us this was an intentional decision to show that while the brothers all have their own identities and roles, they are united as one community—brothers even in death. In another act of symbolism, each headstone lies flat on the grass, rather than pointing upright, to represent humility.

The stark beauty of Saint-Sixtus's church. *Caroline Wallace*

The lush grounds of Saint-Sixtus. *Caroline Wallace*

Inside the church we witness what is perhaps the most clear example of austere architecture we see at any of the abbeys we visit. The Trappists do not believe in worshipping in spaces cluttered by heavy religious iconography, preferring no distractions between them and God. With a wood beam ceiling, simple brick walls, and pools of light entering the room from geometric panels of stained glass above, the church is stark, but it is by no means glum. This is our final stop with Brother Godfried, who introduces us to our next guide, Brother Joris, one of the brothers working in the brewery.

A WORLD-RENOWNED BREWERY TAKES SHAPE

Brother Joris has been at Saint-Sixtus for more than twenty years. Before he became a monk he worked as a Belgian federal police officer. Now he is the head of quality for the brewery and one of two people in charge of overseeing production. He wears prescription Ray-Ban eyeglasses and carries a cell phone in the pocket of his robe because, while he may be a monk, he still has a business to run.

The Westvleteren monks were, and continue to be, physically and intimately involved in the brewing of beer. There is a subtle twinge of pride in Joris' voice as he explains this. While most Trappist abbeys have a monk who oversees a staff of layman brewery workers, Westvleteren has developed an innovative structure to keep the brothers involved in every step of the process. Brewing, sales, quality control, and production are all handled by monks, but each brother is paired with a layman counterpart to help with the work, a system that has proven necessary because the monks have

The Westvleteren brewhouse. *Caroline Wallace*

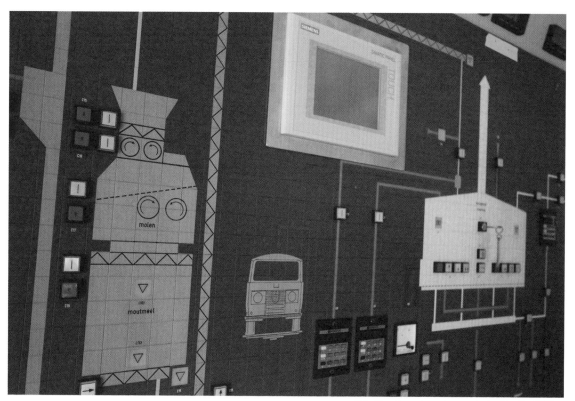

The Brewhouse's analog controls. *Caroline Wallace*

A glimpse of Westvletern's open fermentation, which takes place behind closed doors. *Caroline Wallace*

Quality control is the chief concern of the Westvleteren lab. *Caroline Wallace*

always had to leave the brewery frequently for a heavy schedule of daily prayer sessions.

The monks of Westvleteren brew three beers: the refreshing Blond, the dark and strong 8, and the evenly dark but stronger 12. From brewing to bottling, after which the beers undergo a secondary fermentation, the process takes six to ten weeks, depending on the beer. Though the brewery is state of the art in many ways, the brewhouse still has a manual control panel that looks a little retro compared to the gleaming tanks but gives the brewery a human touch. The beers are unfiltered, unpasteurized, and are still fermented in open vessels, a traditional method that sets Westvleteren apart from other Trappist breweries, as well as from most other breweries in the world. The yeast isn't actually a house culture, but comes from the larger Trappist brewery of Westmalle; a member of the Westvleteren team drives up once a week to retrieve it from the brewery. As we marvel at the sight and smells of the open fermentation process, Brother Joris tells us about just how far the brewery has come since it was started 175 years ago.

The brothers of Saint-Sixtus purchased their first brew system on June 15, 1838, only a few short years after the monastery was founded. The system, which cost them 919 francs, was referred to in the abbey's purchase records as "an old brewery," likely indicating the equipment was bought used. Saint-Sixtus received a brewer's license the next year and conducted their first official brew at that time (*International Trappist Association: Westvleteren*). The beers brewed during these early decades were not for commercial sale, though; it was not until 1871 that they first sold beer to the public.

According to *Brew Like a Monk: Trappist, Abbey, and Strong Belgian Ales and How to Brew Them*, Westvleteren modernized after WWI, growing to a scale comparable to the other Belgian Trappists at the time. The abbey even owned several cafés where their beers were served to the public and a truck to deliver the cases. In 1945, in the wake of WWII, Abbot Deleye made the decision to severely cut back production so the monks could focus on their spiritual lives. Going forward the commercial beer was to be brewed under contract license rather than at the abbey itself, though the abbey would continue to brew in small quantities for the monks, guests of the abbey, the neighboring brewery owned café In de Vrede (which continues to operate as a tasting room and restaurant across the street from the abbey to this day), and for sales at the abbey.

The commercial license for the beer was sold to Saint Bernardus, down the road in Watou, Belgium. Now a household name for beer lovers across the globe, Saint Bernardus was not a brewery but a cheese factory at the time, started under the guidance of monks from Mont-des-Cats, who lived in Watou for a couple decades to escape anticlerical attitudes in France. The cheese factory continued to operate commercially after the monks returned to France in 1934. Westvleteren's brewmaster Mathieu Szafranski became a partner in Saint Bernardus and got the brewery off the ground brewing the original Westvleteren recipes. Over the decades the beers were sold under a variety of different brand names, including "St. Sixtus" and eventually just "Sixtus."

In 1989 the brothers of Saint-Sixtus renovated a modern brewhouse back at the abbey and soon thereafter ended the contract deal with Saint Bernardus, returning exclusive use of the brand to the brewery, which has continued to brew beer exclusively for sale from the abbey and In de Vrede with no outside distribution.

The beers the Westvleteren monks brewed in the 1990s look a little different than the varieties they offer today:

> Until 1999, when Brother Filip created the new Westvleteren Blond to mark the opening of the remodeled In de Vrede café, the beers could be called simply 4, 6, 8, and 12, and were identified by the color of their caps: green, red, blue, and yellow, respectively. At different times they were known as Dubbel, Special, Extra, and Abt, respectively. All but the 4 were dark. The new Blond replaced the 4 and 6, and the monks may drink it with their lunch. (Hieronymus, 2005)

Throughout the 1990s, Westvleteren beers developed a solid reputation, particularly the Blond, which became the go-to brew for not only the monks but also the frequent flocks of cyclists passing through the region.

Nothing could have prepared the monks for the reputation their beer was about to gain once the Internet got hold of it. In 2002, RateBeer.com, which had only been around for a couple years at this point, released its first annual ranked list of the "World's Best Breweries." Sitting at number 1 on that list was Westvleteren.

In the years that followed, RateBeer started putting out these "Best Of" lists for individual beers, and while all of Westvleteren's brews were well received, it was the 12 (affectionately known as Westy 12) that became a star, receiving the title "#1 Beer in the World" several times.

Soon "RateBeerians" and folks who heard about Westy 12 through the media attention that followed were lined up around the block at Saint-Sixtus, eager to take home bottles of this legendary brew that could only be legally acquired at the abbey. A Belgian TV crew even captured footage of a fistfight breaking out in line over the beer.

The story goes that the monks were so frustrated by this influx of beer hunters that they called up RateBeer's Executive Director Joe Tucker to let him know what a problem this accolade had caused. The people wanted more beer, but the monks, not swayed by fame, profit, nor even Internet beer reviews, had no intention of making it.

The abbey devised a call-in system to deal as best they could with the heavy demand. Customers interested in purchasing cases of the beer would now need to make a reservation over the phone to secure their allotment—often set at just one case—in advance and sign up for a pickup window. License plates would be tracked, and after a car made a pickup, it would not be permitted to do so again for at least sixty days. The phone system and the new restrictions were still not enough to thwart the barrage of thirst for Westvleteren:

Exterior view of the brewery and its surrounding buildings. *Caroline Wallace*

An on-site barn houses empty crates of Westvleteren beer. *Caroline Wallace*

Exterior view of the Westvleteren packaging hall. *Caroline Wallace*

A simple crucifix lies on a windowsill at the brewery. *Caroline Wallace*

Crates of Westvleteren beer. *Caroline Wallace*

The infamous Westvleteren phone. *Caroline Wallace*

When the call system was introduced the volume was so high that the local exchange crashed, forcing the monks to switch to a national high-capacity number. At their peak as many as 85,000 calls are made per hour, of which only about 200 get through during a two-to-three-hour window. (*Belgian Trappists Overwhelmed by World's Best Beer Tag,* 2014)

As a result Westvleteren beers, particularly the 12, started to show up on the black market. People sold it on the Internet for outrageous prices, and even today you can still walk into touristy shops in Brussels and see Westies being sold by the single bottle, straight out of the brewery's signature wooden crates, at a 600% markup. This does not jive well with Brother Joris, who recognizes the beer is scarce and wants it all to go to the people who are passionate enough to call in time after time to secure a reservation or come drink at the café. Furthermore, the Rule of Saint Benedict, which informs the monks' way of life, suggests that monastic communities should sell their goods at a reasonable price, which when you consider the price of most export and craft beers today Westvleteren really does. During our visit cases of twenty-four are selling for just 32–42 euros, depending on the beer, and the brothers of Saint-Sixtus are careful to make sure all of their customers know it is not to be resold. The policy is clearly spelled out on the brewery's website, and there is even a reminder printed on customer receipts. Alas, some people continue to skirt the rules.

The only legal way fans have ever been able to purchase the famous 12 outside Westvleteren came when the brewery needed to bring in more income to cover some of the outstanding funds from the new cloister construction. A need within the community was the only thing that could have caused the monks to brew more beer, so over the course of two years they maxed out capacity, brewing in extra shifts to create more batches of 12. They packaged the beer in thematic gift boxes decorated with a dark stone graphic resembling the new cloister, and the gift packs soon came to be called brick boxes, or simply bricks. Each brick box contained six bottles of 12 and two souvenir Westvleteren glasses. The bottles were actually labeled with a simple Westvleteren 12 design directly on the glass, unlike their naked counterparts sold from the abbey.

The bricks were released in two phases. First, 90,000 went out to retailers in Belgium. Then, by the end of 2012, another round had made it around the world, with 15,000 ending up in the United States. Shelton Brothers Imports, who handled the American distribution, was criticized for their decision to grant Total Wine & More exclusive rights to sell the gift packs in some states, meaning other retailers and consumers who did not live near a Total Wine missed out. No matter how Shelton Brothers handled the limited supply, there could never have been enough Westvleteren on US soil to go around though, and the gift packs were sold out before they had barely warmed store shelves.

"We are probably the brewery with the largest group of disappointed potential buyers in the world," Brother Joris told Dan Shelton when he appeared on Shelton's "High and Mighty Beer" podcast just after the US release.

At any rate, the release was a highly successful one strictly in terms of sales for Westvleteren, and the brothers were able to pay off the construction debts.

Today, as we tour the abbey, the monks are back to a smaller production schedule, though a state-of-the-art new packaging hall means a team of brothers is no longer required for hand bottling days. All those brick boxes have either been drank or retreated to the backs of beer nerds' cellars. The call volume at the abbey has dropped considerably since the days of crashing phone exchanges, but demand is still higher than the monks are willing to meet. It is still a treat to get through on the phone lines and receive an allotment of cases, but Westvleteren is also packaging in six packs that are sold sporadically at In de Vrede when production allows.

As we continue our tour with Brother Joris, a monk rides by on a bicycle. "That's Brother Michael," Brother Joris says. "Our head of sales."

Brother Joris takes us in the direction Michael is headed, the drive-up area where lucky cars will soon be permitted to enter for the day.

Westvleteren's shiny new packaging hall. *Caroline Wallace*

The packaging line. *Caroline Wallace*

Eager customers begin to gather at the abbey gate. *Caroline Wallace*

We can already see a small group of twenty-somethings congregating outside the gate in anticipation of their precious rations. We snap some photos of them and Brother Joris remarks it may be the very first time someone has actually taken a photo from the inside looking out, rather than the other way around.

A glass of Westvleteren Blond on the back patio of In de Vrede. *Caroline Wallace*

THE BEER
Westvleteren Blond (5.8% ABV)
The lightest beer in the Westvleteren family, Blond is delicate and soft, while still presenting some light, grassy hop notes and yeasty esters. The beer is a tremendous example of fineness for those willing to let themselves be wowed by a more humble brew.

Westvleteren 8 (8% ABV)
This Belgian Dubbel delivers notes of stone fruit, caramel, vanilla, and clove, along with a discernible touch of hop bitterness. A dry finish balances out some up front sweetness to make for a well balanced drinking experience.

Westvleteren 12 (10.2% ABV)
This full-bodied Quad has drawn worldwide acclaim for its complexity and exceptional flavor. Caramel sweetness, luscious dark fruit notes, leather, and tobacco combine for a sensuous drinking experience. Some prefer it fresh, while others age it for years. Best to get a full case and decide for yourself.

TRAVEL TIPS
While tours of the brewery and abbey of Saint-Sixtus are not permitted there are still many stellar reasons to visit. The first comes for those lucky enough to make a reservation

The exterior of In de Vrede café. *Caroline Wallace*

in advance to purchase crates of beer. Reservations are currently made over the phone, and prices and availability are updated on the brewery's website as they change.

For those who can't get through on the notoriously congested phone lines, there is still the opportunity to visit In de Vrede, the abbey-owned café next door. Here all three beers can be sampled on site, along with simple snack offerings in an atmosphere that is often bustling with beer nerds and locals alike. Six packs of beer are sporadically sold from the café gift shop as production allows, so make sure to scope it out when you arrive, as you may still be leaving with some liquid souvenirs after all. Just make sure not to leave those beers in plain sight in your vehicle. According to Brother Joris, the beers are in such demand that on a few rare occasions thieves have smashed in car windows in the lot to snatch people's hauls.

Across the street at the abbey visitors can experience a small slice of serenity by visiting the abbey's Lourdes Grotto and a humble pilgrim's chapel.

It is possible to stay overnight at the abbey's guesthouse for up to one week. Guests are expected to respect the silence of the abbey and refrain from speaking during meals. They must also attend prayer services, which begin at 3:30 a.m. While spending a week at Saint-Sixtus can be a life-changing experience, for these reasons it is not recommended for the casual beer traveler, but instead for those looking for a spiritual retreat.

AREA ATTRACTIONS
While the quaint abbey of Saint-Sixtus may feel isolated, there are actually many other world class beer destinations in the region surrounding it.

Saint Bernardus and Het Brouwershuis
For the ultimate beer nerd holiday, consider sleeping steps away from St. Bernardus Brewery, where an on-site bed and breakfast known as the "Brewer's House" boasts twelve reasonably priced rooms. Saint Bernardus is just a twenty to twenty-five minute drive from Westvleteren, meaning both stops can

The bustling interior of In de Vrede café. *Caroline Wallace*

easily be squeezed into an afternoon of beer-fueled fun.

Het Wethuys

Another charming accommodation choice in the area is Het Wethuys, a quaint seven-room bed and breakfast with an in-house restaurant decorated with striking, dramatic photographs taken during hop harvests in the region. As an extra thematic touch, each guest room is named after a different hop variety. A short walk from the hotel on the Watou's small town square, guests can view a historic brewer's statue honoring the town's rich beer heritage.

Hopmuseum Poperinge

Just fifteen minutes south of Saint-Sixtus, in the center of Poperinge, sits a museum dedicated to beer's most famous ingredient: hops. For just a few Euros visitors can view historic photographs, documents, models, and audiovisual elements that tell the story of the region's hoppy history.

De Struise Brouwers

Just ten minutes down the road from Saint-Sixtus, beer travelers will run into another world class brewery. Known for high alcohol, experimental brews like Black Albert and Cuvée Delphine, De Struise Brouwers' brewery and tasting room are within the walls of an old schoolhouse accessible through a courtyard entrance totally obscured from the road. In-the-know beer drinkers intrepid enough to find their way here during Saturday tasting room hours are rewarded with an impressive variety of on-site and take-away beers.

De Dolle Brouwers

Another twenty-five minutes or so down the road from De Struise is De Dolle Brouwers, which opens its tasting room doors to visitors on Saturdays and Sundays. This colorful, rustic space is decorated in the same wacky, whimsical style as the brewery's beer labels, which are illustrated by brewer Kris Herteleer. This is truly one of the most unique breweries we have ever seen.

WESTMALLE

Abdij van Onze-Lieve-Vrouw van het Heilig Hart
Van Westmalle (Westmalle Abbey)
Brouwerij Westmalle
Westmalle, Belgium

Westmalle illustration, *Jessica Deahl*

08. Westmalle

Abdij van Onze-Lieve-Vrouw van het Heilig Hart Van Westmalle (Westmalle Abbey)
Brouwerij Westmalle
Westmalle, Belgium

Set in the stretching meadows of Flemish Belgium, Westmalle Abbey is situated on a few sprawling acres of dairy farmland several hundred feet off the main road out from the town of Malle. It is not uncommon to see visitors adventuring around the perimeter of the abbey and through the expansive forestlands either on foot, on bike, or by horseback as the Westmalle Community's herd of cows lazily graze in the pastures nearest the road.

The drive out to Westmalle feels exceptionally quiet after leaving the bustle of Ghent's city limits. While we have spent the weekend exploring Ghent, Westmalle is much closer geographically to Antwerp. It is a Monday afternoon, so when we stop at Café Trappisten across the street for a late lunch, there is a small crowd quietly enjoying the

menu of croque monsieurs, pastas, and Trappist cheeses.

It's a lovely, open tavern. Originally the building was a grocery store that was rented from the community and partially converted into a café in the early 1920s. It has since expanded into a much larger restaurant and event space. We order the sampler of cheese and a round of beers: Westmalle Dubbel, Westmalle Tripel, and a Westmalle "Half & Half" that combines both beers like a blended Belgian black and tan.

Westmalle has developed quite a mystique during our travels. Many other Trappists link back to this large but removed monastery. We are unsure what to expect from this community and from the larger-scale brewing operation they run to support their monastery, but are anxiously awaiting the

The interior of Café Trappisten is airy but cozy. *Caroline Wallace*

chance to discuss their quiet presence at so many monasteries.

As we near our appointment with Phillipe Van Assche and Brother Benedikt Van Overstraeten, we leave the café, cross the mildly busy street (complete with a bus stop servicing the abbey's other visitors), and walk down the monastery's main cobblestone boulevard.

A long, straight road lined with shrubbery and evenly spaced and well-tended mature trees directs visitors to the Westmalle Abbey gate, which is simply but beautifully

The walking trails that lead to Westmalle Abbey are lined with large, established trees. *Caroline Wallace*

decorated with busts of the Virgin Mary. Behind the gate visitors can see the gigantic bell tower denoting the cloister where the monks spend the majority of their days in silent study and prayer.

The physical space that holds the brewery was completed in 1934. As renovations and additions have occurred due to the brewery's growth over the years, architects have the unique challenge of matching the style of the existing buildings while also creating a contemporary design for the additions. The result is a cohesive and beautifully austere landscape that is a quiet record of the abbey's history, from its somewhat medieval citadel-like wall, to the stark ornamentation on the walls of the gates and the abbey itself, to the beautiful brewery offices completed in 2004. There is a sense of purpose behind each building and design aesthetic.

The underlying tone of Westmalle Abbey is peacefully industrious. Compared to other Trappist Abbeys we visit on our journey, Westmalle was downright bustling with people enjoying the afternoon in the forests and on the trails. In the brewery area there

The gates at Westmalle have beautifully detailed sculptures adorning them. *Caroline Wallace*

Westmalle's brewery offices feature a window shaped like the beer's logo. *Caroline Wallace*

were multitudes of laypeople working in the offices, more than we have seen in any one place at most of the abbeys we've had the opportunity to explore.

The abbey is named after and in the area known as Westmalle. Westmalle and its eastern counterpart Oostmalle are two halves of the twin city Malle. Divided in the Middle Ages, in 1979, the two halves were reunited under the town's original name, Malle, as it is known today.

Malle is situated in the Campine region of the Flemish province of Antwerp. Campine encompasses the land within the northeastern border of Belgium, but also covers the southeastern-most parts of the Netherlands. Known historically for its extensive moors, evergreen woodlands, and wetlands, the name Campine derives from the Latin word for "region of fields." Remarkably flat with poor, sandy soil, there are few large cities in the region and the area is isolated and quiet. For this reason multiple abbeys, including Westmalle Abbey, have been established in the area.

In recent years the region has become a popular destination for tourists in search of relaxation and peace. A number of retreats and bed and breakfasts have replaced the old farmhouses of generations past. There is also an extensive network of cycling trails that draw many visitors to the area.

HISTORY AT WESTMALLE ABBEY

Between the sixteenth and eighteenth centuries, Malle, as well as numerous other villages in the Campine region of Belgium, was plundered and severely besieged. After the havoc brought on by Dutch and Spanish troops during the Eighty Years War, outbreaks of the Bubonic plague, and the inevitable dire straits the region endured while recovering from the turmoil, by the 1580s there were only twenty-three surviving families in the town of Westmalle. They lived in hiding for more than four years at Westmalle Castle.

It was two centuries later that the first Cistercians made their way to Westmalle. The impetus for this exodus began in 1780s France.

The church at Westmalle is far removed from the bustle of the brewery operations. *Caroline Wallace*

Young priest Father Augustinus de Lestrange Dubosc was scoped to be the future coadjutor bishop to Jean George le Franc de Pompignan, Archbishop of Vienne, a position that would essentially seat him as the co-head of the diocese in all but ceremonial precedence. The prospect of taking on the responsibilities of a bishop greatly disconcerted de Lestrange. He shortly thereafter severed all ties with the modern world and entered La Trappe Abbey, in the French province Normandy. La Trappe Abbey is the origin of the Order of Cistercians of the Strict Observance, the very earliest Trappist community (*Augustinus De Lestrange Dubosc*).

In the violent aftermath of the French Revolution, a decree of the National Assembly, which was led for a time by Archbishop Jean George le Franc de Pompignan, went out suppressing the religious orders of France, including the Cistercian and Trappist communities.

"A lot of religious people and monks were murdered [at that time]," Brother Benedikt Van Overstraeten says. "It was a genocide against the religious and blue-blooded people."

Artifacts from centuries past at the abbey are now on display outside the abbey shop. *Caroline Wallace*

The decree of the national assembly and subsequent violence against the Catholic orders forced the twenty-four brothers of La Trappe Abbey to flee for Switzerland in 1791. Led by novice master Dom Augustinus, they settled in an ancient Carthusian monastery called La Valsainte. Under the order of Dom Augustinus in 1794, a number of monks were sent away from La Valsainte to establish new communities in Spain, Italy, and Belgium. It was a portion of this group of monks that were the first to build the priory at Westmalle.

The brothers chose to settle in Westmalle specifically at the request of the Bishop of Antwerp. They had originally intended to leave for America.

"It tickled their imagination to go there," Brother Benedikt says.

The bishop offered them a small farm during their stay in Antwerp named Nooit Rust, which translates to "Never Rest" in English and symbolizes the unremitting manual labor on the farm and in the fields, and the monks' ceaseless search for God.

For several years regional political woes seemed to slowly taper off, and the monks were able to successfully establish and maintain the farm and monastery.

The reprieve was short-lived, and within a few brief years the monks realized they had not escaped the dangerous impacts of shifts in governmental power entirely. In early 1815 Prince of Orange-Nassau Willem Frederik—also known as Willem I—proclaimed the Netherlands a freestanding kingdom at the direction of the Congress of Vienna. This proclamation merged the Protestant country of Holland with the Catholic Flemish area of Belgium, causing an immense amount of turmoil between the Dutch and Belgians. It also jeopardized the fate of many Belgian Catholic orders. Westmalle was in jeopardy of closure, but since the priory held a craft school at the time, Willem I recognized it served a purpose for the community outside the monastery's walls, so in 1822, he granted the priory legal status.

Despite the murky sociopolitical landscape surrounding the monastery, the community's numbers increased. In 1830 Belgium was recognized as its own kingdom; as a result of the newfound peace, many young men flocked

Westmalle's small guest chapel is a quiet place for visitors to practice their faith.

to the monastic lifestyle in what is today known as the "Restoration." As more brothers chose monastic life, the monastery expanded. In 1836 the monastery became an abbey, meaning it fell under the control and guidance of an abbot. In 1842 the abbot and the community were given legal ownership of the land. Westmalle's inaugural abbot, Dom Martinus, also led the effort of constructing the abbey's first small brewery to staunch the thirst of the burgeoning community.

A detailed image of one of the sculptures of a saint outside the gates of Westmalle. *Caroline Wallace*

EVOLUTION OF THE WESTMALLE ABBEY BREWERY

Brother Benedikt tells us the regulations of Abbot Armand Jean le Bouthillier du Rancé, founder of the Trappist Order in the seventeenth century, allow brothers of the order to drink a single glass of the popular regional beverages of their abbey's area with their meals. When Dom Rancé established these regulations at La Trappe Abbey, the regional beverage of choice in Normandy was cider, but Belgium has a deep and long withstanding love affair with beer, so the brothers began brewing in 1836, and enjoyed the first brew of Westmalle Trappist beer on December 10.

Initially brewed to sustain the community's need for beer with their meals, it wasn't until 1856 that the brothers began to sell beer at the gate of the abbey. Local demand for the beer increased steadily, so to meet that demand the brewery underwent two expansions in 1865 and 1897.

"This flourishing period [for the abbey] lasted until the second World War, 1940," Benedikt says.

Westmalle's yeast in a branded chalice.
Caroline Wallace

Brother Benedikt tells us that after World War I and especially after World War II, there were significant changes throughout Europe. One of the foremost changes in culture came in the form of communication and industrialization. Globally, the religious communities of the world were coming into crisis as young men who once would have been drawn to the church found callings in the expanding industrialized secular world.

Despite the decrease in young men coming into the monastic way of life, in terms of industry the beer the monks were producing was gaining popularity. This commercialization of Westmalle Trappist beer in the early twentieth century helped support not only the immediate Community at Westmalle, but also other outreach efforts. These efforts included financing a daughter house in the Belgian Congo and establishing a Trappistine abbey in the nearby town of Brecht.

The beer itself also underwent several changes as the market evolved during the mid-twentieth century. Belgium had a ban on dark liquors up until the 1980s, an effect of the American prohibition. The lack of dark spirits in the Belgian market inspired Westmalle to increase the alcohol by volume (ABV) of the beer, and it took on a darker, more complex flavor. To achieve this, the brothers began brewing with higher quantities of malt and sugar in their new copper kettles.

Despite the growing demand for the refined suds, by the 1950s, the brothers at Westmalle were fearful of overexpansion of

The brewers at Westmalle use a French hop for their beers.
Caroline Wallace

Westmalle's brewhouse is as beautiful as it is practical, with large frosted windows lighting it. *Caroline Wallace*

the brewing operation. They requested that the laymen operating the brewery find more automated solutions to meet market requests, rather than expand the brewery more. Their gentle reminder was "This is a monastery with a brewery, not vice versa." Production was capped from then on at 120,000 hectoliters (100,000 barrels) annually.

Today the beers are brewed largely the same way they have been for hundreds of years, following all of the stipulations established by the International Trappist Association. The old brewhouse is filled with warm light that reflects happily off the copper tanks and white and navy tiles throughout the room.

As we walk through the space, our gracious guide speaks about the fate of the special French malt Westmalle brewers use. Once it has released all of its sugars in the mash tun, the grain is sent to the pastures for the cows. The cows seemingly appreciate the sweet, wet malt and the cheese that is made with their milk benefits from those special flavors as well.

For the most part, Westmalle Abbey ferments their beers to the same time and temperature standards as their surrounding Belgian and Dutch Trappist communities. The beers are bottle conditioned with a second addition of yeast and sugar, matured in the bottle on premises for a few weeks, and then sent out into a world hungry to taste them.

FARMING AT WESTMALLE ABBEY

Westmalle Abbey also operates a cheese-making facility and the original farm to support the community.

The first monks at the monastery established the farm in 1794. They were some of the first to pursue farming on a commercial level in the area, as the region had historically been known as an agricultural wasteland. Similar to the origins of many Trappist activities, the farm was initially established as a means of self-support for the community, but as it took hold and began to produce excess, the brothers shared the bounty with the small villages and towns surrounding the abbey.

"A lot of active monasteries had farms. We had a couple cows for milk, farming land for grain, vegetables, and potatoes, all for self-supporting," Brother Benedikt says.

While the brothers once carried out arable and dairy farming, they downsized the agricultural endeavors beginning in 1932 and allowed the brewery to become the main source of income for the community, but the community continued raising livestock.

Brother Benedikt tells us it is common practice for abbeys to keep livestock. It is thought of as enriching to the lives of the brothers, as well as the animals.

Currently, the community's herd consists of mainly Groningse Blaarkop cows, a centuries-old breed known for their sturdiness, high fertility, and high protein levels in their milk. The surrounding lands make an ideal home for the cattle with long plains and

One of Westmalle's herd of cattle that produce the milk necessary for the community's cheese program. *Caroline Wallace*

The expansive farmlands that surround Westmalle Abbey. *Caroline Wallace*

meadows. Westmalle cows are treated with the highest standards in care. They are milked twice daily, and they spend the warm summer days basking in the expansive pastures surrounding the monastery's walls. As a result, at one point in the monastery's history over 10,000 hectoliters (260,000 gallons) of milk were being produced annually.

Having such well tended animals producing milk with such a protein-rich composition made cheese making a natural secondary vocation for the brothers at Westmalle. Begun in 1860, the cheese-making process has been overseen by the brothers of the community for more than 150 years using milk from their own cows. Unpasteurized, full-cream milk is processed and the resulting cheese is pressed, washed, and matured by hand to produce small batches of semihard cheese. The monks sell the cheese at the gates of the abbey.

Cheese production is the industry within the abbey that the monks have the most day-to-day influence on. They take a more administrative role with the brewery. Between 1992 and 1998, most of the board of director seats have transitioned from brothers to laypeople. In 1998 a charter was drawn up by the community outlining all standards and stipulations the brewery was to adhere to, but even today a brother is still directly involved on a daily basis in the cheese factory.

THE COMMUNITY

Today thirty-three brothers live and work at Westmalle—the biggest community in Belgium and Holland—numbers not particularly staggering historically.

The view outside the brewing facility at Westmalle Abbey. *Caroline Wallace*

"There were once over one hundred monks here and the average age was much lower," Brother Benedikt says.

While the average age of the community has decreased in the past two years, this is due to several deaths of brothers who were over ninety years old, rather than the result of an influx of young brothers.

"Young monks are not coming to the monastery. People who are now coming into the monastery are already past thirty years old. Of people who come from other orders, the average age is near seventy, with many over eighty," comments Brother Benedikt.

Brother Benedikt speaks in greater detail about the effects global industrialization had on the Trappist communities regarding growth. Shortly after World War II there were still young people coming into the orders from around the globe. There was so much of an augmentation that a large monastery was built in Vaalbeek, Belgium, to educate the young generation of monks. Sadly, by the time the monastery was completed, there were few young monks left to teach. Today the monastery in Vaalbeek is

used by laypeople for contemplation and religious education.

Brother Benedikt shared his personal journey to the community while we spoke at Westmalle. He was born and raised in Dendermonde, Belgium, a town in East Flanders between Ghent, Antwerp, and Brussels. In 1980 he came to Westmalle Abbey after beginning his secular career as a civic engineer. He continues his engineering vocation at the abbey today as part of his work within the brotherhood. He plays a role in everything from the design of the labels for the beer to the architecture and layout of new buildings.

"It's not obligatory to have a certain background. There are brothers who come from specialized backgrounds [focused on hands-on trades] and brothers with several degrees from multiple universities," Brother Benedikt says.

As it was in the case of Brother Benedikt's past learnings, the education and experiences a man carries with him into the faith are readily utilized once he commits himself to the monk's robes. It is also possible

A small ornamentation atop a pillar at the entrance of Westmalle Abbey. *Caroline Wallace*

The final steps in the Westmalle brewing process are bottle refermentation and packaging for distribution. *Caroline Wallace*

for novices who are in the process of becoming a monk to complete full degrees in multiple fields before completing the journey into the community. Once a person has fully committed themselves to a particular community, he is also permitted to earn degrees while at the monastery, but only theological ones.

Continual education is an integral part of the brothers' lives. Many hours of each day are devoted to what they refer to as "personal study." These periods of study are observed in silence and contemplation. Early on, a monk focuses on a foundational theological education until he feels he is able to embark on a personal level in this philosophical and theological mental journey. This deeper personal analysis is central to the life of the monks.

THE BEER

Westmalle Dubbel (7.00%)

Westmalle Dubbel is a traditional Belgian Dubbel style ale. Commonly sold in 33 cL bottles and perfectly portioned for the familiar Westmalle goblet, the Dubbel pours a dense, rich brown with ruby highlights and

A full chalice of Westmalle Dubbel. *Caroline Wallace*

an incredible amount of head. The subsequent lacing of the head works its way down nearly the entire glass. The aroma of the Dubbel is fruity and dark, with notes of roasted brown sugars; dark pitted fruits like cherries, plums, and figs; and herbaceous esters. The satiny initial mouth feel gives way to a highly carbonated finish. The flavor opens up with dark robust malty notes and dark fruit and travels through to a dry, slightly spicy finish.

Weighing in at 7.00% ABV, this recipe has remained wholly unchanged since 1926, although the monks have been brewing dark beer since the brewery began operating in 1836. Like all Westmalle beers, it undergoes a second fermentation in the bottle that allows the finished beer to continue evolving in flavor as it ages. In addition to the 33 cL bottles, the Westmalle Dubbel is also sold in 75 cL bottles and is the only Westmalle beer distributed in kegs to external hotels, restaurants, and cafés.

Westmalle Tripel (9.50%)

Westmalle Tripel is a lighter, higher alcohol beer. Called the "mother of all Tripels," the Westmalle monks began brewing this beer in 1934. By 1956, they had perfected a recipe that, like the Dubbel, has gone practically unaltered since.

Also available commonly in 33 cL and 75 cL bottles, the Tripel is a hazy straw color with a billowy white head. The aroma is reminiscent of ripe bananas, citrus, yeast, and spiced pears. The flavor begins with notes of slightly sweet fruits and earthy spices but gives way to an underlying bitterness similar to orange peel. It has a medium body and high carbonation. While the 9.50% ABV is present in the taste up front, as the glass warms the flavors mellow and the alcohol is likewise tamed.

Westmalle Extra (4.80%)

While the Extra is not available for public sale, it is most similar in style to a Belgian Pale ale. It is the lowest alcohol Westmalle offering, weighing in at 4.80%. The Extra is brewed only twice a year for the brothers and guests in the guesthouse to drink with their meals.

TRAVEL TIPS

While the abbey's church and internal grounds are kept largely private for the brothers, visitors are welcome to enjoy the property that abuts the monastery walls. There are copious walking trails that are heavily traveled during the warmer seasons, and visitors can buy Westmalle cheese and other Trappist wares from the gift shop at the gates of the abbey. The community sometimes accepts individuals searching for spiritual retreat into the guesthouse, where these individuals can pray and live alongside the monks for a few days, but special permission must be obtained; it is not a typical vacation, but more a challenging exercise in spiritual connectedness and contemplation.

For those seeking to try the beers from Westmalle Abbey, Café Trappisten is as close as one can get to the brewery. The café is across the street and features a large food and beverage menu, including the cheeses produced at Westmalle and the Dubbel, Tripel, and a special blending of the two. It

Daily specials are written out on a chalkboard at Café Trappisten. *Caroline Wallace*

also offers a momentous amount of indoor and outdoor seating for solo visitors and large groups alike.

AREA ATTRACTIONS

In the town of Malle and surrounding areas, there are more opportunities to experience the history of the region. There is Renesse Castle in Malle, which serves as a museum and concert venue, and a multitude of forests and trails visitors can walk or bike. Malle is also only a forty minute drive from Antwerp, making it an easy half-day trip if you are staying in the city proper and looking for a quiet retreat.

ZUNDERT

Abdij Maria Toevlucht (Abbey Mary Our Refuge)
Trappistenbrouwerij de Kievit
Zundert, the Netherlands

Zundert illustration. *Jessica Deahl*

09. Zundert

Abdij Maria Toevlucht (Abbey Mary Our Refuge)
Trappistenbrouwerij de Kievit
Zundert, the Netherlands

We are nearing the end of the Belgian and Dutch leg of our trip. Driving through the picturesque forestry of the Dutch province Noord Brabant, our thoughts are focused on the days ahead. After our last Dutch interview we will travel the rest of the day through Germany to Engelszell. After a morning interview at the Austrian Monastery, we will be heading to Rome the next afternoon. Although we are each a little preoccupied about the next three days—the last seventy-two hours we will spend in Europe—the beauty of the landscape around us draws our attention back to the most pressing matter at hand: our interview with the enigmatic brothers of Maria Toevlucht Abbey.

Maria Toevlucht Abbey's history with brewing is the shortest we have encountered up to this point in our journey. The community made the decision to begin brewing only seven years prior to our visit, so the brothers largely responsible for moving the monastery's financial dependency away from agriculture and toward brewing are still active in the community. It is with them we will be speaking today, and the possibility of understanding the creation of a new recipe from the monastic point of view has us incredibly excited.

As we near Abdij Maria Toevlucht—known colloquially as Zundert due to its location just outside the town of the same name—the ancient trees cast the roads in a warm green light as the morning sun trickles its way down through their leaves. The land is still and untouched. While all of the communities we have visited have been relatively far outside the reach of modernity

The welcome center and abbey shop at Abdij Maria Toevlucht. *Caroline Wallace*

and urbanization, the tranquility of this morning and the loveliness of the woodlands surrounding us give us insight into the benefits of such isolation. It is easy to let the mind wander, to be contemplative in such a still place.

We pull into the small, deserted lot outside the monastery's visitor center and see our interpreter and a strong, stately cloaked brother quietly conversing outside, awaiting our arrival. We step out of our car and make our introductions. Brother Christiaan van Opstal welcomes us and ushers us through the visitation center of the monastery into the open courtyard beyond.

We walk for several minutes around the grounds, seeing no people, but countless rabbits enjoying the morning's warmth. Brother Christiaan takes a call on his cell phone and informs us Brother Guido, his colleague in the brewery and our second interviewee this morning, will be joining us in a few minutes. He is tending to the bees in the community apiary, of which he takes primary responsibility. Brother Christiaan leads us around the exterior of the brewery and

explains the building was renovated for brewing only a few years prior. For much of the community's history it was a cattle stable. Looking at the exterior we note the signs of wear and age have not been totally removed. They add character and stand as tokens of the brothers' hard work and the tolls of time the community has weathered.

Brother Christiaan, who has a background in psychiatry and spent a fourteen year sabbatical outside the monastery walls as a counselor and nurse, brings us indoors into a conference room. As we settle in, a tall brother with kind eyes and a warm handshake enters the room. He introduces himself as Brother Guido and apologizes for his late entrance.

Both monks are industrious and purposeful in all we see them do. While they are quiet, it is evident they are striving to be as helpful and open with us as possible. We sit as Brother Guido serves us coffee and Brother Christiaan goes into the history of the abbey.

The guesthouse and church at Abdij Maria Toevlucht. *Caroline Wallace*

HISTORY OF MARY OUR REFUGE

The abbey was formed in 1900, when a band of twelve monks from Zundert's mother community the Abbey of Our Lady of Koningshoeven built a refuge house for French monks who were forced to leave their country because of new anticlerical legislation. It is from this history that the abbey gets its formal name Abbey Maria Toevlucht (Abbey Mary Our Refuge).

Being a heavily Catholic region of the Netherlands, a Zundert villager nearby donated an old farm to the monks to establish a life for themselves. After this first small piece of land was cultivated, the community of twelve expanded the grounds through careful purchases and additional donations from surrounding towns.

Even with the gracious gifts of their neighbors, the brothers had a daunting task ahead. The grounds were not prepared to be heavily farmed, and it took an incredible amount of dedication and effort to cultivate the land to a profitable state. They began tilling the land to support root vegetables like potatoes and beets. By 1950 the brothers had moved their industry primarily to raising livestock.

As the land flourished, so did the community. By the end of World War II upwards of eighty monks called the small monastery home. To offset the overcrowding, ten brothers traveled from the walls of Zundert to help another Trappist monastery in need. At the end of the war, when the French and German borders were renegotiated, a German monastery found itself displaced on newly named French lands. The German brothers were forced out by the war-torn inhabitants of the surrounding towns, and the monastery was left abandoned. The Dutch brothers of Zundert moved into the monastery and brought it back to life as a functioning community.

This story is tragic on many levels. Trappists have a deep connection, not only with God and their exploration of

This image was taken in the early 1900s and shows members of the community tending to livestock outside the abbey farm named "de Kievit." *Courtesy of Abdij Maria Toevlucht*

Inside the chapel where members of the community worship several times each day. *Caroline Wallace*

spirituality, but also with the landscape of their chosen community.

"It is an essential part of our rule to stay at the same place. We chose this abbey, this place, and this community," says Brother Guido.

Currently sixteen brothers call Zundert home. They are all between forty-two and ninety-four years of age, which is a fairly accurate representation of community demographics at the majority of Trappist abbeys worldwide.

"When people enter the monastery nowadays, they've had a social life prior to entering. In the past they were seventeen, eighteen, nineteen years old. Now they are twenty-five, thirty, or even older. The structure of social life and church life isn't as clear as it was several years ago. People are going their own way more than they were in the past," Brother Christiaan says.

The community kept its own farm from 1900 to 2010. While the land surrounding their monastery is still theirs, they no longer use agriculture as their main source of revenue. With the help of local and national subsidies, they have repurposed the land to be used as a nature preserve. Cattle still roam the premises and are tended to, but they are not put to any sort of work. In the community's century-long history relatively little has changed until 2003, when the brothers received groundbreaking news.

DEVELOPING THE BREW

The impetus for change at the monastery came from a report from external economists at the start of 2003 who had evaluated the local Community of Zundert.

"They told us 'at the moment, we don't see any problems, but in the future, you will need to develop a new source of livelihood' because the farm alone could not continue sustaining us," says Brother Christiaan.

This was a large cause for alarm, for it was not just the brothers that depended on the farm for income. Separate from the community's needs are several charities that depend on the brothers' income. These charities span from nonprofits in Africa to funding medical research for mental and physical health concerns. Locally, in light of the global economic crisis of 2008 and the results it had in Holland, there are pockets of hidden minor poverty riddled throughout the country. To provide assistance, the brothers established outreach charities that fight poverty using funds the community raised.

Armed with the information that there was imminent need for new industry and ever aware of the responsibilities the abbey had not just to the brothers but the countless lives touched by their income through charitable causes, in 2008, the community began thinking about what sort of source of revenue they could establish. The term "brewery" was mentioned. Other monasteries had made a steady stream of revenue from brewing activities in the past, and with the lull in agricultural needs the brothers had space for a new brewing facility, so the process of brainstorming and planning was underway.

Such a dramatic shift in the foundation of life at Zundert required much planning. Early on, a coalition of nine brothers was tasked with researching and developing an initial

Candles are lit with prayers to the Virgin Mary.
Caroline Wallace

Brother Christiaan and Brother Guido explain the process of defining the tone of the beer with the help of a word-mapping exercise. *Caroline Wallace*

plan for brewing as a sustaining industry. They were continuously reporting their findings and next steps to the rest of the community. When a plan was finalized in early 2008, there was a democratic vote among the sixteen brothers. The vote was overwhelmingly in support of making the brewery a reality.

The coalition was then tasked with defining the characteristics of the beer that would set it apart in the market.

"It was very important to us to say we have our own recipe, not a copy from another; our own unique taste of Zundert that is representative of our community," notes Brother Christiaan.

The process of identifying the notes of the beer began with no beer at all, but with an in-depth word map laying out words that spoke to the community itself. Visually laid out, there were larger themes referencing the province of Holland they call home and the history of that land, references to nature, and words about life at the monastery. Motifs like challenge, contemplation, grey, silence, desert,

nutritious, roots, and hope all make their way into the map.

One of the most meaningful words on the map is a very old Dutch word, *Weerbarstig.* This translates roughly in English as "difficult" or "eccentric." The beer the brothers hoped to create was not one for everyone. Conceptually it had very specific, almost eccentric taste. They sought for it to be slightly niche and not easy drinking. One would need to take time with this beer. It is a beer for contemplation and a beer meant for sharing with friends.

With the word-mapping exercise complete and a tone defined, the brothers were ready to bring in help matching their ideas for their future product to a taste and style, but they could not take these steps alone. They called in a brewmaster and a beer connoisseur. Together the team began tasting, which they did often and with much vigor. They tasted beers of varying styles and beers of different strengths. They tried beers with such extreme tastes they were unlike anything the nine brothers had tasted before.

Over and over again they tasted until they could pinpoint characteristics they appreciated. Then the brewer began mixing different beers based on their feedback and reactions. For more than two years this continued until an agreement was reached among the brothers.

The color, ABV, and general flavor characteristics were defined enough to begin working out the more nuanced notes of the beer, so the brewmaster started making proof of concepts in the form of forty liter batches of beer. To extract a variety of flavors, he hopped each batch differently from the next. Naturally, the brothers were required to taste the test batches and they excitedly obliged.

"It was a very happy time," says Brother Guido.

In 2013, when the brothers were satisfied with the finished product, the brewer began scaling the recipe for their production-sized batches, being mindful of the changes in flavor that could take place. As each batch today uses upwards of 1,000 kg of malt, this was no small undertaking. He also took this opportunity to educate all the brothers involved in the creation of beer on best brewing practices.

It was during this time Brothers Christiaan and Guido were completing an internship of sorts at another Trappist monastery producing beer. There they learned the tradition of brewing Trappist beers on a large scale, and through this hands on experience they acquired the skills necessary to head the beer program at Zundert.

The monastery's brewhouse was also being completed during this whirlwind of planning and early execution. The original cattle stable had very high ceilings, making it an ideal candidate for the large lagering tanks that would need to occupy it. A wall was expanded out during the remodel and was rebuilt with oversized windows to allow the early morning sun to flood the brewhouse.

The end effect is breathtaking. The diffused light gleams off the stainless steel brewing equipment. The chalky white walls and vaulted ceilings are supported by exposed beams. The sole source of ornamentation comes in the form of a delicately painted statuette of Saint Arnold hung on a support in the center of the

The cattle stable was renovated into the abbey's brewhouse in 2013. *Caroline Wallace*

The vaulted ceilings around the brewery's fermenters emulate the vaulted ceilings inside the abbey's church. *Caroline Wallace*

Brewing equipment at Abdij Maria Toevlucht is situated in front of massive windows to utilize natural light in the brewhouse.
Caroline Wallace

brewhouse. The tone is demure and understated, not unlike the Trappist churches we have already experienced. The monks have designed for themselves a working space as familiar as the sanctuary they spend nearly half of each day worshipping in. It is a seamless addition to the landscape, and the spiritual energy of the space is palpable.

Brothers Christiaan and Guido are wholly responsible for the daily operations within the brewery. As the community has an aggressive production schedule and a demanding agenda

A small sculpture of Saint Arnold is practically the only form of ornamentation in the brewhouse where Zundert beers are made. *Caroline Wallace*

in terms of mass, studies, and contemplation, balancing the hours of the day becomes very important.

They wake well before 4:00 a.m. on brew days to begin the boil in time to make it to their 4:30 a.m. service. It is during this time their automated systems monitor the time and temperature at which the sugars are being extracted from the malt. There are three distinct temperatures that must be reached and maintained to extract the sugars fully. Later, once the wort has reached the appropriate gravity, the spent grain will make its way to a local fertilizer company, keeping the brewhouse's waste production low.

At 6:30 a.m. they return to add their hop additions to the boil. Zundert's beer uses a unique varietal of hop for bitterness and taste that is added into the mash in two separate stages of the boil. These hop additions, along with a secret bouquet of herbs, blend together for the unique "Weerbarstig" taste that differentiates Zundert from its brethren brews.

At 7:00 a.m., the brewmaster checks on the status of the day, but for the most part he serves as a quiet external advisor. Brothers

Brother Guido and Brother Christiaan pose inside the brewhouse. *Caroline Wallace*

Christiaan and Guido will repeat the brewing process twice more in a day for four consecutive days to fill their six lagering tanks.

Once the beer is in the lagering tanks, it will spend roughly a week in active fermentation. Then the beer will be cooled and lagered at this lower temperature for at least two weeks before the yeast is pitched and the beer is moved to a bottling facility.

Because Zundert is in an ecological safe haven the area has limitations as far as industrial possibilities. Brewing is permissible, but the additional noise and traffic produced from an on-site bottling line and distribution center would violate governmental decree. While the local government was willing to help the community's investigations of the feasibility of putting a brewery on the grounds, the procedure necessary was arduous and the scrutiny was extensive. Seeking additional permits for packaging on site was simply not feasible, which truthfully suited the community just fine.

"There is a saying 'Monks brew to live. They don't live to brew,'" notes Brother Christiaan.

While some of the abbeys we toured described feelings of satisfaction and a sense of peace while listening to the deafening clatter of a bottling line, the brothers here prefer the hum of the wind, the hops of their cotton-tailed neighbors, and the gentle buzzing of the bees in the apiary. They partner with a local bottling facility that handles the final addition of yeast and sugar at the beer's final packaging step.

Despite packaging taking place off site, the brothers were very much involved in the branding and marketing story of their beer. They initially began this process by looking at existing Trappist beers; they did not want to copy anything. They wanted to be distinguishable from the other beers. Being a small brewery operation, custom bottles were out of the question, so to accomplish this via another route their layman graphic designer proposed a predominantly purple color plan in their labeling to make a clear distinction. Additionally, the brothers concurred that the color purple added a sense of intrigue and mystery to the product's story.

The exterior of the church at Abdij Maria Toevlucht. The arches over the windows play an important role in the branding of the beer brewed at the abbey. *Caroline Wallace*

Imagery was incredibly important to the brothers, so they brought in an advertising agency to distill icons really representative of the monastic way of life. The ad agency that helped them did so by taking photos of the grounds. During their time at the abbey the photographers noted an architectural element that was aesthetically pleasing and significant above every window of the main building: a keystone. A detail oft overlooked by brothers who called the monastery home, this keystone shape depicted on the face of the bottle arching over all other design elements on the label is a longtime symbol of premiere importance within a structure. It is, literally and metaphorically, an integral element of a larger structure that locks all other elements in place and allows the structure to be self-supporting.

Another key piece of iconography in the design is the graphic illustration of a Kievit. The original name of the farm was tied to the pasture-dwelling bird tucked away in the grass surrounding the monastery. Including its likeness in the design was a very purposeful nod to the abbey's history, as well as its natural surroundings.

Being a brand new Trappist brewery in the company of ancient names like Orval, Chimay, and Rochefort, the go-to-market plan for the community was incredibly important. The brothers listened carefully for the reception of the public as they released their first beers in 2013. During the first six months there was a lot of excitement brewing around the beer, and they couldn't keep up with demand.

After the demand died down slightly, the brothers began to consider the sustainability of their brand and their product, specifically contemplating the key elements that would continue their success. They are now in the phase of executing those plans to build the brand. They often get information about the perception and reaction to the beer from distributors to keep up-to-date feedback. They also recruit independent external advisors from whom they get pertinent market research.

As far as hands-on marketing pushes, the abbey's distributor is in charge of the marketing now. They often have sit-downs to talk strategy, but it is not the monks' way to be hosting tastings and putting on events.

Of the sixteen brothers in the community—even of the small coalition of nine that carefully laid all of the plans for the brewery—today only two head up all things beer. They handle the brewing and meetings with distributors, advisors, and the brewmaster. They regularly report to the other brothers, but they are the head brewers.

For so small and remote an abbey, it is difficult to understand the brothers' choice to keep the brewing responsibilities tied to the community, rather than solely relying on the efforts of laymen. Upon deeper consideration, one can see they built this concept from the ground up. Every element of the beer was conceptualized, vetted, and realized by the community. They want to keep the idea of the beer close to the community and strive to be very involved.

In the span of a year the brewmasters can produce roughly 2,500 barrels of beer in a space that could accommodate no more than 4,000 to 5,000 barrels annually. They do not plan to expand the beer offerings or their output capacity. Right now they dictate the amount of beer they produce based on the fiscal need of the community and the charities they want to support in a given year. This capacity is enough to sustain their lives so they do not desire to increase production. Again, monks brew to live; they do not live to brew.

THE BEER

Zundert Trappist Beer (8.00% ABV)
The brothers at Zundert are plenty occupied brewing just one beer for the foreseeable future. It is a variation of a Tripel that incorporates a proprietary blend of spices and herbs. It pours an orange-amber with a cream-color head. It has a distinct nose of clove, spice, malts, green fruits, and a tinge of alcohol. This beer has a honey, bready flavor with spicy notes and a medium body, a creamy mouth feel, and a surprisingly dry finish. It is available in select accounts in Belgium and the Netherlands in 330 mL bottles.

Inside the abbey shop. *Caroline Wallace*

TRAVEL TIPS

Zundert is not open for tours of the brewery, but has a well-stocked abbey shop and a visitor center mainly used for religious consultations.

AREA ATTRACTIONS

There are multitudes of walking trails surrounding the area, so visitors can make the most of the lush landscape. Also, in the city of Zundert travelers can visit the Vincent Van Gogh House. Van Gogh was born in the town, and his childhood home is now an immersive museum featuring some of his early works, as well as a rich history of his life.

STIFT ENGELSZELL

Engelszell Abbey (Stift Engelszell)
Stift Engelszell Trappist Brewery
Engelhartszell an der Donau, Austria

Illustration of Engelszell Abbey. *Jessica Deahl*

10. Stift Engelszell

Engelszell Abbey (Stift Engelszell)
Stift Engelszell Trappist Brewery
Engelhartszell an der Donau, Austria

A picturesque drive along the precariously brimming banks of the Danube delivers us to the next stop on this adventure: Engelszell Abbey. The only Trappist monastery in Austria, Engelszell lies in the hilly upper region of the country, just a stone's throw past a sleepy, unmarked border shared with the south German state Bavaria. Our German interpreter, Alina, points out that a nondescript gas station we pass with little regard serves as the locals' in-the-know border marker.

Since Engelszell was founded at the tail end of the thirteenth century in this remote village there have been many changes at the abbey, including a full-scale renovation in the eighteenth century and the introduction of a commercial brewery in 2012. Most of those changes have been in reaction to the ways the world has insisted on changing around Engelszell.

When we meet up with our friendly guides Jennifer Jungwirth and Abbot Marianus Hauseder at the abbey they tell us about this evolution.

A TURBULENT REFUGE

The story of Engelszell begins in 1293, when Bernhard of Prambach, Bishop of Passau, founded it as a Cistercian monastery. Two years later Cistercian monks from nearby Wilhering Abbey came to Engelszell, and the burgeoning monastery's numbers strengthened and prospered more or less peacefully for centuries.

The Protestant Reformation took a considerable spiritual and financial toll on the abbey throughout the sixteenth century. In

The breathtaking church. *Caroline Wallace*

Aerial view of Engelszell Abbey along the Danube. *Stefan Reicheneder*

A glass entombed skeleton is draped in gold and jewels. *Caroline Wallace*

Countless works of art adorn the church of Engelszell Abbey. *Caroline Wallace*

Countless works of art adorn the church of Engelszell Abbey. *Caroline Wallace*

Countless works of art adorn the church of Engelszell Abbey. *Caroline Wallace*

Stift Engelszell. *Caroline Wallace*

1618 Engelszell's mother house Wilhering Abbey intervened and was committed to turning the monastery around. Another hardship for Engelszell came in 1699 on Easter Sunday, when a fire broke out at the monastery, destroying much in its path. The task of rebuilding once again put the monastery in a precarious financial state, and it struggled for decades until Abbot Leopold Reichl, Engelszell's last abbot as a house of the Common Observance, was appointed in 1746 and vowed to turn things around. Reichl oversaw the rebuilding of the abbey's church from 1754 to 1764. The church was constructed in a magnificently ornate Rococo ("Late Baroque") fashion with a towering 76 meter (249 ft) steeple and precious works of art from Johann Georg Üblher, Joseph Deutschmann, and Bartolomeo Altomonte.

Just one year after construction on the church was complete, Holy Roman Emperor Joseph II came into power. An enlightened monarch who believed in the modernization of the Catholic Church, Joseph had little patience for the seemingly old world tradition of contemplative monasticism. During his reign Joseph dissolved somewhere between 700 and 800 monasteries, and in 1786 Engelszell joined that list. After the monks disbanded, the monastery fell into private, secular ownership and served many different manufacturing and residential functions over the course of the following years.

But in 1925 the abbey returned to its monastic roots when the private owners sold it to a group of Trappist monks of German descent who came from the great Oelenberg Abbey in France. Their abbey had suffered immensely during World War I, so Engelszell now became these monks' priory and their refuge. The monks carried the tradition of brewing beer with them from Oelenberg and produced their own brews at Engelszell up until 1929, when their old equipment gave out (Rail, 2012). They also began distilling spirits to support the priory, including "Magenbitter" (stomach bitters), which would go on to become their most popular product. The priory was elevated to the rank of abbey in 1931, and along with the distinction came the appointment of the group's former Prior,

Gregorius Eisvogel, to the position of abbot. For a brief time in the years that followed, the community flourished.

Tragically, the promise of Engelszell Abbey's new beginning happened to rub up against one of the darkest periods in human history. In 1939 the Gestapo seized Engelszell, forcing the seventy-three monks who called the abbey home to vacate. Their rationale for seizing the abbey was allegedly "For statements against the security of the state" (*Stift Engelszell Trappistenbier*). Five brothers were arrested and sent to Dachau, about 20 kilometers (12.5 miles) north of Munich. By the time Dachau was liberated by American troops six years later, four of those five brothers had lost their lives.

Prisoner's barracks at Dachau. *T/4 Sidney Blau, 163rd Signal Photo Company, Army Signal Corps*

That same year, twenty-three of the original seventy-three monks returned to Engelszell. They were joined by fifteen more Trappist monks who were displaced from their monastery in Yugoslavia (Bosnia). In the years that followed the monks operated an assisted living facility that had been started at the abbey during the war. (This facility still exists today, but it has been moved to a new building and is operated by the international nonprofit Caritas.) In 1957 they restored the damaged nave of their church and commissioned Fritz Fröhlich to paint an expansive and impressive mural across its ceiling to match the baroque style of the rest of the sanctuary. Though the ornate church is not in line with the simplicity of traditional Trappist architecture, it has

Abbot Marianus Hauseder of Stift Engelszell. *Caroline Wallace*

served as a popular tourist attraction, drawing more than ten thousand visitors from all over Europe every year who come to admire the fresco. (The monks have a separate, smaller church where they conduct their regular daily prayers, but they do lead a public mass in the large church every Sunday.) Thanks to the work of the monks, the scar of WWII is no longer visible on the abbey, but the community has not gone without its hardships.

BEER: AN ECONOMIC BOOST

As members of the Engelszell community acknowledge, "The monks who worked to reestablish monastic life and its economy on the large, historical site of Engelszell Abbey form a Community which has steadily grown smaller, while the necessary tasks and

challenges have only continued to increase" (*Stift Engelszell*).

Up until 2012, the abbey was mainly being supported by liquor and honey production from the on-site distillery and apiary, but the income from these industries was simply not enough to cover some of the abbey's serious expenses, including new repairs that needed to take place on the church. That is when Peter Krammer, owner of the family-run Brauerei Hofstetten a few towns away, suggested the monks start a brewery of their own. Beer could be the economic boost the abbey needed, but they first had to figure out how they were going to brew it.

"We were lucky," Abbot Marianus says as he leads us to the brewhouse. "We already had an

The modern brewhouse. *Caroline Wallace*

empty building we could use for the brewery, so that reduced the cost of construction."

Over the course of the next year Krammer worked with the abbey to plan the brewery, and they settled on a partnership that has Abbot Marianus overseeing the brewery in accordance with the International Trappist Association guidelines while a brewer from Hofstetten comes over once a week on brew day. We happen to be at Engelszell for one of those brew days, and as we enter the small yet modern brewhouse, the sounds of work and smells of wort are in the air.

The Hofstetten team collaborated with Engelszell on the recipes for their beers. Each of Stift Engelszell's three beers has been named after an influential figure in the community's history. The first, Gregorius—a dark ale brewed with local honey to honor the abbey's tradition of apiculture—is fittingly named after the first elected abbot, Gregorius Eisvogel. "His unbridled enthusiasm, dedication, determination, and above all his faith in God were highly instrumental in reviving the monastery along the river Danube to a pulsating new life" (*Stift Engelszell*).

Next came Benno—a Belgian style farmhouse ale also brewed with honey— named for the Bosnian monk Benno Stumpf, who became abbot of Engelszell in 1952. Stumpf oversaw the renovation of the cathedral and monastic buildings and thus earned a very important space in the community's heart.

Finally, the abbey's third and newest beer, the lighter Nivard, is popular with the Austrian locals. It is named for another one of the abbey's influential Bosnian brothers, Father Nivard Volkmer. Volkmer also came to Engelszell after WWII and held various roles, including two years as the abbey's Superior. In 1991 Volkmer was called back to Bosnia to serve as abbot of the monastery he grew up in. He served until 2002, when he was able to retire from his role and return to Engelszell. He passed away in 2014, and the beer bears his name to honor his memory.

As we exit the brewhouse, a van pulls up. Like a lot of small breweries in Europe, Stift Engelszell does not bottle its own beer. A bottling line would be too large, too costly, and too noisy for the small abbey at this point, so the beer is pumped into the tank of this van and taken to the bottling partner that Hofstetten also uses. An extra dose of honey is added to the beer at this time that will serve to kick-start secondary fermentation when the beers land in their bottles.

These beers are important for the Engelszell Community, not just because they were able to make repairs to their church because of them or because the abbey will need a new roof next year, but because the brewery serves as an investment in the abbey's future.

THE BEER

Gregorius (9.7 % ABV)

This Belgian style strong dark ale features a nutty, fruity, herbaceous aroma coupled with pronounced honey and chocolate flavors. A slight, sour, cherry-like tartness accompanies an otherwise dry finish for a complex drinking experience that fuses just enough traditional Belgian character with an experimental Engelszell twist.

Benno (7% ABV)

Sometimes characterized as a Belgian Dubbel, while other times called a Belgian style farmhouse ale, one thing that is certain is that Benno is a unique beer brewed with honey. It is a little hazy, a little funky, a little fruity, and a little herbaceous. The beer starts sweet but finishes dry with a hint of spice.

The beer is transported to an off-site bottling facility to minimize expense and noise at the abbey. *Caroline Wallace*

The beauty of Engelszell. *Caroline Wallace*

Nivard (5.5% ABV)

The newest of Engelszell's beers, Nivard is a bright, herbaceous beer with a medium body and a touch of hop bitterness. It is golden in color, and it tastes pretty darn golden too.

TRAVEL TIPS

The main reason tourists visit Engelszell Abbey is to gaze at the Collegiate Church, an opulent rococo masterpiece of a building adorned with an impressive fresco, countless statues, and a handful of glass-entombed skeletons draped in gold and jewels. While the church is open daily for visitors to peruse at their leisure, guided tours can be arranged in advance for the full experience.

Another welcoming feature of Engelszell Abbey is its gift shop, where beer and liquor can be purchased, along with a wide variety of monastic products.

AREA ATTRACTIONS

To experience Engelszell Abbey you first have to get to Engelszell Abbey. The best bet for accommodations is in the nearby German university town of Passau. Nicknamed the "city of three rivers," Passau sits amongst stunning Lower Bavarian countryside where the Danube intersects with the Inn from the south and the Ilz from the north. There are a handful of solid, low-cost accommodation options here, including the Panorama House Hostel, which provided us with a clean, safe stay and a stunning view. For a traditional German meal in Passau accompanied, of course, by copious liters of beer, Altes Bräuhaus is a convenient and cozy stop where an evening can pass in a festive flash.

From Passau, Engelszell Abbey is a zippy 30–35 minute drive by car, or there's the option to opt for a longer, meandering bike ride along the scenic Danube.

The land surrounding Engelszell is heavily forested. *Caroline Wallace*

A house on the Engelszell property offers shelter to refugees. *Caroline Wallace*

A collection of abbey buildings. *Caroline Wallace*

The Klosterpforte (abbey shop) where many monastic products, including beer, can be purchased. *Caroline Wallace*

A small, whimsical castle adorns the abbey grounds. *Caroline Wallace*

TRE FONTANE

Abbazia delle Tre Fontane (Tre Fontane Abbey)
Tre Fontane Brewery
Rome, Italy

11. Tre Fontane

Abbazia delle Tre Fontane (Tre Fontane Abbey)
Tre Fontane Brewery
Rome, Italy

Nearing the end of our journey, we sit on the train platform at Munich Central Station nearly swallowed by our own luggage. One does not travel to some of the most coveted brewing regions on earth and leave without beer, so we have garnered a rather extensive collection of bottles and memorabilia purchased and gifted along the way. Now equipped with an extra carry-on bag each to accommodate our acquired cargo, we spent the night before carefully wrapping and tucking away our precious bottles inside clothing and plastic bags. We recall some earlier advice we received about traveling lightly through Europe, say a silent prayer, and zip up our parcels. Stuffed into a glorified closet (the train's sleeping compartment) for the next twelve hours, we are road-weary but excited. The announcement in 2015 of an

eleventh official Trappist beer meant an unexpected addition to our trip: Tre Fontane in Italy.

There is almost no place in the world as steeped in history and tradition as Rome. The "Eternal City" is over 2,500 years old, one of the oldest continuously occupied cities in the European Union. Rome houses Vatican City, the geographical center of Roman Catholicism and seat of the pope. It is also one of the origins of Western civilization, a major city of influence in the Italian Renaissance from which the Coliseum and Michelangelo were born, and current home to three million people.

We are only going to spend the next twenty-four hours in the city, a whirlwind pit stop outside of the Belgium/Netherlands/ Austria abbeys. Tre Fontane is geographically

Church of Santa Maria Scala Coeli at Tre Fontane Abbey. *Jessica Deahl*

and culturally distinct from the other Trappist locales we visited (save the abbey at Spencer, Massachusetts) and very "Italian" in the most endearing way. Our train arrives hours late to the station due to some unknown delay we missed during our slumber. We exit the convoy, lugging about one hundred pounds of luggage each, and step into Roma Termini train station. Way behind schedule, we are stressed, irritated, and unfortunately late for our interview. We drive through packed and unfamiliar Roman roads to the Tre Fontane Abbey, about a 6.5 mile trek from the city center.

A private drive down into a small valley leads to an unexpectedly quiet sanctuary and provides reprieve from the flood of strangers and tourists we have just encountered. Despite the ancient city growing around it, Tre Fontane maintains the same peaceful space required for contemplative life as all Trappist abbeys. Now centuries old, this place was once chosen as a Cistercian abbey for its placement far from the city. The Arch of Charlemagne marks the entrance to the abbey, a two-story monument framed by two towers. A relief of the Virgin Mary adorns the external facade, along with a plaque commemorating two Roman Jews who took refuge at the abbey in 1944.

As the distractions of our hectic morning dissolve we are put especially at ease when we meet Sergio Daniele, the spokesman for the new brewery and former head of the liquor factory of Tre Fontane. He is a sharply dressed, warm, inquisitive man with a captivating sense of humor. Mere minutes into our interview he offers us strong espresso and Trappist chocolates on the house. It's beginning to feel a lot like Italy.

PEACE IN THE HEART OF ROME

We walk the abbey grounds with Sergio, getting to know Tre Fontane Abbey. He speaks of the abbey like an old friend, full of pride and optimism for the future. The land is peppered with palm trees, reminding us of the symbol for hope we had seen on Rochefort's crest a few weeks earlier. The abbey receives hundreds of thousands of visitors each year, not yet for its world class beer (as we'd seen at previous abbeys), but for its significance as a Christian pilgrimage destination.

Tre Fontane Abbey is visited as the site of St. Paul's martyrdom. *Courtesy of Tre Fontane Abbey*

The location's history dates back to Biblical times. According to the New Testament, Roman Apostle Paul spent his final days in Rome. After being accused of not observing Jewish law in Jerusalem, Paul traveled to Rome to appeal to Caesar as a Roman citizen. Though not written in the Bible, Christian tradition holds that Paul was martyred with Saint Peter during the reign of Nero (around 64 AD). It was written in Greek (*Acta Petri et Pauli*) in the fourth and fifth century: "Peter and Paul, received their sentence, were driven from the presence of Nero. Paul was led in chains to a place three miles from the city, escorted by three soldiers of noble families. . .He was beheaded at the holding of Aquae Salviae, near the pine tree."

A twelfth century belief holds that Saint Paul's severed head bounced three times on the ground and a spring miraculously arose from each contact. Thus Aquae Salviae became Tre Fontane (Three Fountains). The Aquae Salviae was most likely rural for many years, and it is speculated it housed a wealthy Roman family's villa for a time. The area is below sea level and offers an abundant presence of water. The first official document naming the place came from Pope Gregory (590–604), stating the proceeds of the Basilica of St. Paul would go toward keeping the lamps on at the Apostle's tomb day and night (Montanari, 1967, 74).

A document reveals that Greek monks from the Roman province Cilicia inhabited the Aquae Salviae by 649. In the mid-seventh century this site of Saint Paul's martyrdom was officially acknowledged to be a sacred place, and it became and remains an important pilgrimage destination in Rome. In 998, the monastery was abandoned. Decades later, during Pope Gregory VII's tenure, it was given to the Benedictines of St. Paul.

A schism in the church during a Papal election in 1130 marked the arrival of Cistercians to Tre Fontane Abbey. On February 14, 1130, two popes were simultaneously elected in Rome: Innocent II and Anacletus II. The latter won the support of a majority of the cardinals, and Innocent II found refuge in France. There he made a strong ally in Bernard of Clairvaux, an abbot and primary builder of the reforming Cistercian Order at Cîteaux. When Anacletus II died suddenly in 1138, Innocent II went back to Rome and took on his position as pope. Though the schism ended in his favor, he punished those who had voted against him. He was especially hard on the Benedictines of St. Paul, taking the monastery at Tre Fontane from them to give to St. Bernard. On October 25, 1140, a group of Cistercians arrived at Aquae Salviae, making it the thirty-fourth "daughter house" of Clairvaux (Montanari, 1967, 75).

According to the Cistercian Order, the layout of monastic spaces is to follow specific organization and established architectural rules. The monks who arrived at Tre Fontane demolished and rebuilt buildings over the next few decades to turn what was a Roman monastery into a true Cistercian abbey. It was, from this point on, known as an abbey. By the end of the thirteenth century Tre Fontane was one of the most powerful abbeys in Rome. This was facilitated largely by the abbey's first abbot, Bernardo Paganelli, becoming pope in 1145.

Over the next few centuries the abbey alternated between periods of prosperity and difficulty. Napoleon's occupation of Rome in 1808 led to its closure in 1812. The monks were sent away and the community's assets confiscated. Tre Fontane was still a beloved pilgrimage destination, and Pope Leo XII attempted to revive it in 1826 by handing it over to a group of Franciscans who did little to improve upon it. Pope Pius IX intervened and brought Trappists to the abbey in 1868. This revival coincided with the 1,800th anniversary of Saint Paul and Saint Peter's deaths. Polluted waters were cleaned and malaria was eradicated. Archeological digs at this time revealed fossilized pine logs and some ancient coins dating back to Nero's age, further confirming the site as the place of Saint Paul's martyrdom "near the pine tree" (Montanari, 1967, 76).

We move along a tree-lined street past the churches of Saints Vincent and Anastasius and Santa Maria Scala Coeli to the church erected to commemorate the martyrdom. It has a brick and travertine facade and the portal, cornices, and capitals that remind us we are in Rome. Sergio directs us to a painting of Saint Peter, a copy of "Crucifixion" by Guido Reni (1575–1642). The saint asked to be crucified upside down, as he did not wish to be killed in the same manner as Christ. A small column, said to be the one on which Paul's head was placed, sits in the corner. Along the wall are the actual Three Fountains from tradition whose sources have been covered since the 1950s, as the water was too polluted to drink.

Being surrounded by this depth of history is not lost on us. Even with weeks of European travel and abbey visits behind us, the chance to stand in this place, with this story of humanity dating back two thousand years, is a rare and meaningful privilege. An unexpected gift of our Trappist beer adventure is access to these types of destinations, and we could not be more honored to visit them.

THE ABBEY TODAY

Tucked behind this publicly visited site is the inner cloister, reserved only for monks. "You see how many tourists are here?" Sergio asks. "It is very closed. Why? Because that is the character of the monks. We are in the center of Rome. If you are in a very small village you can be open. We have to be conservative. It is good, but it is very difficult."

He remarks that a lot of people, believers or not, visit and find sanctuary here. Though tourists are not accommodated within the abbey, visitors seeking spiritual retreat can book day- or week-long stays in guesthouses, though space is limited.

The abbey grounds are rich with botanical harvest. Six varieties of eucalyptus trees— planted by the Trappist monks—were thought to be a cure for malaria. The monks noticed that wherever the plant was located, malaria did not exist. In truth, eucalyptus acts as a natural insecticide by reducing large quantities of water. The prevalence of eucalyptus at the abbey today has made it an accessible asset for various liqueurs and eventually the abbey's first beer—a Tripel. Oranges grown on the land are also used in liqueur, an apiary yields Trappist honey, and abbey-grown olives are processed into olive oil to be packaged and sold.

The new logo developed for Tre Fontane, announced as the eleventh official Trappist brewery in 2015. *Caroline Wallace*

The gift shop at Tre Fontane Abbey sells an assortment of monastic goods. *Caroline Wallace*

Two stores operate on the premises for visitors to purchase these monastic goods: one owned by the abbey and another family-owned café and gift shop across the parking lot. As with all Cistercian Orders of the Strict Observance, the monks at Tre Fontane produce only enough to meet their needs. However, maintaining a centuries-old abbey in the heart of Rome comes with some very particular needs.

"It is a lot of work to maintain this place," Sergio explains. "These buildings are very old. If you want to make any kind of restoration, you have to call upon all the appropriate museums and historical preservation offices. Everything you want to touch here is expensive. If it costs one euro to build a wall, here it costs ten euros. . .we are a work in progress, all the time we are a work in progress." He pauses. "Let's have a beer, huh?"

THE BREWERY

Today they are brewing. We pass loads of fragrant spent grain on its way to feed local farm animals and enter the brewery, which houses a modest but impressive 10 hL

stainless brewhouse in a newly constructed building in the rear of the complex. Though the end product is overseen by the abbey's Father Danilo, laymen are employed by the monks at Tre Fontane to brew the beer and they are hard at work. The smell inside the brewery is immediately unique. In the midst of the familiar grain, yeast, and hop aromas is a distinct herbaceous scent; it is reminiscent of a spa and incredibly pleasant. Sergio walks over and picks up a mesh bag similar to a giant tea bag filled with eucalyptus. A secret mix of abbey-sourced eucalyptus leaves and hops is added in the boil to give this Tripel a very rare quality.

Only four years prior, the community of monks at Tre Fontane decided to try their hand at brewing beer in a country soaked in wine. The tradition and success of Trappist beer elsewhere was encouraging, so the monks contract brewed a beer off premises to perfect the recipe. Once the experiment proved promising, they invested in brewing equipment and built their own facility within the abbey. The motivation to receive the Authentic Trappist Product label meant the brewery had

Sergio Daniele serves Tre Fontane's
Tripel in the brewery's signature glass.
Caroline Wallace

to carefully adhere to established guidelines. Just six months before our visit to Italy, the brewery at Tre Fontane was fully operational. They brew once per week, two batches per day, to make up to 1,000 hL (850 barrels) per year. That is the maximum annual yield for this rhythm of production, and it is what the community wants. Despite growing interest in the beer, the abbey's motives are not-for-profit, so capacity is kept small.

We sit down with Sergio in his office-meets-distillery in a converted hundred-year-old building that he shares with his wife, Cristiana, and Mauricio, who makes the liquor. The office is stuffed with the trappings of the abbey's brewery and liquor business. Original posters advertising the eucalyptus liqueur in pre-Marxist Russia are hung alongside dusty photos documenting the abbey's architectural history. Warm wood built-ins hold bottles of various liqueurs and curiosities. Sergio apologizes for the lack of pomp and circumstance, but we are officially smitten.

A small community, Sergio's family works closely with the monks to manage all aspects of the brewery. We get the sense they oversee the challenges of a new brewing operation day by day, hour by hour. Business is bustling, and our interview is interrupted many times by the ring of Sergio's cell phone or an unexpected visitor popping by, followed by friendly conversations in Italian. Just the previous week the labeling machine was broken and the community of monks (the oldest of which is ninety-eight) worked feverishly alongside his family to hand label each bottle to meet production needs—a "work in progress," to be sure, albeit a charming one.

Positioned around his office desk for the next few hours, we enjoy the fading afternoon sun and generous conversation as we sample beer. It is the only one of the entire roster of Trappist beers that we had not yet tried, and we are more than eager to change that. Once we are settled Sergio opens a 75 cL bottle of Tre Fontane Tripel and pours it into newly branded tulip glasses. The label bears a simple design reminiscent of the abbey's architecture and feel, with "Tre Fontane— Birra Trappista Italiana" and the coveted

Signage for Eucalittino liqueur, produced from eucalyptus grown at the abbey since 1868. *Caroline Wallace*

Authentic Trappist Product label. The glasses have just arrived, and the abbey plans to produce only four hundred of the specially marked stemware to commemorate each year of the brewery's existence. The majority of our colloquy at Tre Fontane, despite centuries of history that could easily fill a book of its own, revolves around this beer.

The bottle pops as it is opened, a highly carbonated and complex 8.5% ABV Tripel with a rich golden straw color. A bit of spice and herbal notes waft from the glass, only slightly hinting at the alcohol content. It tastes a bit dry and the subtle eucalyptus presence soothes, seeming to add a detectable sweetness to the beer that defies the senses as it warms the body and the boozy backbone reveals itself. Following a sip of the "Eucalittino" eucalyptus liqueur, the beer is reminiscent of sweetened iced tea. "The history of the brewery is six months," Sergio tells us. "But to do this you need 140 years."

The decision to produce a Belgian-style Tripel brewed with eucalyptus by a

The Tre Fontane brewhouse. *Courtesy of Tre Fontane Abbey*

community of monks in the middle of Rome comes with a unique set of challenges, yet this choice was almost obligatory. The Tre Fontane monks have been making the Eucalittino with macerated eucalyptus leaves about as long as Trappist monks have been at the abbey (since 1873).

The abbey needed to develop a beer that could handle the potency of the eucalyptus, so they elected to produce the Tripel—a beer with high enough gravity and body to support it. It is "a little bit Belgium, a little bit Trappist, a little bit Italian," as Sergio puts it. Developing the beer over the first four years of contract brewing took a hefty amount of trial and error, and only now do they feel they have landed on the best recipe. They carefully analyze each batch along with the International Trappist Association to ensure quality. Always hospitable, Orval and Rochefort opened up access to their laboratories for development of Tre Fontane's recipe. The brew's success relies on sourcing the right mix and quantity of eucalyptus leaves, along with carefully monitoring the time they spend in the boil.

"It's like when you make tea; if you leave the bag in hot water too long, it is too strong, too bitter," Sergio tells us. This beer might not be for everyone, but it is exactly what Tre Fontane longed to create.

Trappist monks are nothing if not fastidious, and though this is not always the most business savvy path, the fruits of their labor are worth the work.

"If you want to make a beer that follows the trends of the moment I would never do a Tripel," Sergio muses. "That is also another point, because this is going to be the beer for the next 100 years. Not for the moment. This beer, especially to young people, is a difficult beer. This is not because of business, but that is the main point. It's difficult, huh?"

Though interest in craft beer in Italy is rapidly growing, one is more likely to find a Double IPA in specialty bottle shops in Rome than a Belgian Tripel.

Trappist beers are not exclusively produced to be marketable, but to be honest and reverent to the cause for which they are made. Certainly, the Trappist beers we had enjoyed up to this point were created and

The Tre Fontane brewhouse. *Courtesy of Tre Fontane Abbey*

The brewing at Tre Fontane is lovingly overseen by monks. *Courtesy of Tre Fontane Abbey*

Fragrant spent grain and eucalyptus fills the air during a brew day. *Caroline Wallace*

sustained from recipes that are in many cases hundreds of years old. We can't help but feel as if we are witnesses to history, an important moment adding to the mythos of Tre Fontane.

THE BEER
Tripel with Eucalyptus (8.5% ABV)

This highly carbonated Tripel is a unique and welcome addition to the roster of Trappist beers. The recipe utilizes eucalyptus grown at the abbey since Trappists arrived in 1868. Tre Fontane's Tripel has an abundance of spice and soothing herbaceous notes that balances harmoniously with Belgian yeast and the beer's deceptively boozy body. It is the essence of Tre Fontane—this beer perfectly represents the place it was made.

So far the Tripel is sold in 75 cL and 33 cL bottles around Rome, and just recently to a few other cities in Italy. Bottles are available for purchase at the abbey and at locations around the city. With production as limited as it is, there are no plans to export to the

A monk looks on during brew day. *Courtesy of Tre Fontane Abbey*

Glasses of Tre Fontane Tripel. *Caroline Wallace*

United States. For now visitors will have to make the trek to Rome to try it.

TRAVEL TIPS

Visitors can attend mass in the abbey church. Retreatants can make arrangements via Tre Fontane Abbey's website to stay in a private or double room for one to six days.

The complex is open daily for visitors, and each of the abbey's three churches has varying hours. The monastic shop is open daily selling Trappist goods—including the beer!

The abbey is about six miles from the city center and from approximately one million tourist destinations. The Coliseum, Roman Forum, Catacombs, and St. Peter's Basilica all await! Suffice to say, there is no shortage of things to do and see in Rome. Immediately next to the abbey complex is Hotel Tre Fontane, a three-star hotel that shares a name with the famous martyrdom site.

Bottle design for
Tre Fontane Tripel.
Courtesy of Tre Fontane

SPENCER

Saint Joseph's Abbey
Spencer Brewery
Spencer, Massachusetts, USA

Spencer illustration. *Jessica Deahl*

12. Spencer

Saint Joseph's Abbey
Spencer Brewery
Spencer, Massachusetts, USA

To date, there is only one American Trappist monastery certified by the International Trappist Association as a Trappist brewery. It is situated about an hour outside of Boston, Massachusetts, in a small township called Spencer. The monastery is named St. Joseph's Abbey.

This will be our very last stop on our trip. We are exhausted from travel, injury, sickness, and airport food, as well as a little shell-shocked to be back on American soil. Commonplace conveniences like drive-through banking and twenty-four-hour pharmacies seem funny all of a sudden. We are all looking forward to getting one more glimpse into monastic life before this whirlwind trip is over.

The weather is cool for June, but it is a sunny morning. We make small talk in the car but mostly take in the surroundings. As we drive toward St. Joseph's we note a nearby town is celebrating its 178th anniversary. Red, white, and blue streamers and flags adorn the city center. Farther on there are many heavily forested roads that curve through the countryside, winding up and down over the hills. It is quiet, and we have become a little accustomed to using that silence for contemplations of our own.

We see the abbey gift shop and turn in. We have arrived early to get the lay of the land, so we drive past to tour the grounds. The property feels huge. We drive for several moments before coming to a fork in the road with a demure sign set out to direct traffic. To the right, standing proudly on a sunny hilltop, is the church. To the left is Trappist Preserves, one of the community's sources of

The abbey shop at St. Joseph's Abbey is one of the first buildings visitors encounter. *Caroline Wallace*

revenue, and what we can begin to assume may be the brewery.

We veer left first. There are austere buildings to meet the needs of the preserve factory, a few small loading docks, and offices all shaded by well-established evergreens. The road continues farther back, but we dare not go deeper without invitation. Backtracking to the right, we scale the hill. There is a lovely roundabout in front of the stoic stone church. The architecture is beautiful but subdued. Flowers bloom around the property, and the sun is at its highest.

We head back toward the gift shop to check in, passing a man walking on a trail just off the road. We muse, wondering if he is a brother enjoying the day or perhaps a novice contemplating his choice to submit to this life.

A friendly monk in the gift shop greets us and points us back down the road to the preserves factory. We follow his direction and continue on until our road dead-ends in a parking lot to a large, simply decorated building. A field of clover directly abuts the walkway from the lot to the building. After a passing glance at the flowers, we look down

Fr. Isaac at the tasting table in Spencer Brewery.
Caroline Wallace

The exterior of Spencer Brewery. *Caroline Wallace*

the path to the brewery. Through giant glass windows we can see a towering set of stainless steel kettles. We open the doors and hear the buzz of machinery as a few laymen pass by us.

A congenial, almost cheeky looking monk in glasses soon greets us. This is Father Isaac, who will be speaking with us today. As we make our introductions we laugh about what a relief it is to speak in English without the need for interpreters or fears of missing nuances in translation. He says "Ahh" often as we talk, as if we have stumbled across secrets with our questions, as if we are now co-conspirators here in the brewery. Speaking with Father Isaac is the perfect synthesis between the tranquility of Trappist life we have encountered and all the comforts of home. It is hard for us not to feel as though we have become fast friends with him.

Father Isaac leads us into the brewhouse and begins recounting the community's 190 years of history.

FROM THE BANKS OF HALIFAX TO PETIT CLAIRVAUX

In 1798 a community of Trappists living in the ancient Carthusian monastery of La Valsainte in Switzerland was forced to evacuate when French troops invaded the country. The community initially sought refuge in Russia but was transient for many years (Bertoniere, 2005, 10).

In 1803 Dom Augustine de Lestrange formed a plan for thirty-two brothers to make their way to Canada to establish a permanent Trappist abbey. The plans, so carefully laid, never fully successfully took root.

The group had eventually dwindled down to three brothers on a ship in the harbor of Halifax in Nova Scotia in 1825. They had been shored in the harbor due to a lack of wind, so Dom Vincent de Paul Merle went ashore to collect supplies. While he was away legend tells the wind picked up and the ship departed, leaving the Dom behind. He took that opportunity to form a monastery called Petit Clairvaux (Bertoniere, 2005, 51). This community would evolve over time to become St. Joseph's Abbey, but not without struggle.

Dom Vincent worked tirelessly to establish men in the vocation at Petit Clairvaux. To assist in this effort in 1860, a group of about fifteen monks migrated from Saint-Sixtus Abbey. Life at the monastery improved, and the community grew to more than thirty monks within the next twenty years. They even started a brewing program based on the art the community had carried from Westvleteren.

Tragedy again struck in the start of the 1880s. There was a series of three fires that wreaked considerable damage on the monastery's walls and the spirits of its abbot, Dom Dominic Schietecatte. He was so depressed that he returned to Saint-Sixtus Abbey in Westvleteren with a majority of the brothers.

Six brothers were left at Petit Clairvaux without a leader. Luckily, at the Notre Dame du Lac at Oka in Quebec there was a young, promising Irish monk named John Mary Murphy. Surrounded by French-speaking brothers, Dom Murphy was isolated, and was a great candidate to lead the Community at Petit Clairvaux.

Upon instating his leadership, Dom Murphy and the brothers came to the conclusion that Petit Clairvaux might not be the best location for their community any longer. They packed up a few pigs, cows, carts, and a table that today sits in the brewmaster's office at Spencer, and in 1900 boarded a train inbound for Cumberland, Rhode Island (Bertoniere, 2005, 194).

For the next fifty years the group did well at Cumberland. An influx of brothers after World War II gave them plenty of hands to tend their dairy farm. A beautiful church was built out of blue stone quarried nearby. Fire struck again on the Feast of St. Benedictus in 1950. In a single night a blaze broke out in the guesthouse and burned the entire establishment to the ground.

Faced again with the decision to rebuild or adventure out, the community looked at all the factors at hand. They were short of space due to the number of recruits that joined the monks after the war. The dairy farm wasn't incredibly prosperous, and a local bar had recently been built across the street from the monastery.

The church at St. Joseph's Abbey stands on a hill on the expansive property. *Caroline Wallace.*

Trappist Preserves have been made and sold at the abbey shop for decades. *Caroline Wallace*

"The piano would stop right around 3:30, just in time for morning prayers," Father Isaac says.

The monks decided another move was in order. In 1950 a small group was sent to Spencer to erect a chapel and the beginnings of a new abbey. Dom Edmund Futterer decreed almost immediately after the rest of the group was settled in Spencer that work commence on a permanent church to serve the Community at St. Joseph's Abbey.

In the past, the brothers had made their livelihood primarily with dairy products. This was the initial plan at St. Joseph's as well. The brothers had established a very successful, high yielding herd of cows. These cows were producing so much milk they needed to be milked three times daily. Over time, waking at midnight to milk the cows became a lot for the community to bear. Additionally, the region was transitioning toward agri-business models that did not suit the lifestyle of the monks.

In 1954 the shift toward preserves was made. A brother had already been making and selling mint jelly in the gift shop for some time, so it was a seamless transition to start up Trappist Preserves, a revenue source that the monks still maintain.

In the late 1960s, after a change was issued by the Second Vatican Council regarding the style of Roman Catholic worship robes, a brother at Spencer created an updated design to the traditional cowl worn by the monks. This design simplified the dress and became widely popular across the nation. With that, another stream of revenue was firmly established through the community's liturgical garb manufacturing company, The Holy Rood Guild.

Today fifty-seven brothers call St. Joseph's Abbey home, ranging from historians to the graphic artist responsible for the album art of Barbra Streisand. Of that about 10% are in the middle of their training to become monks. Life has continued for many years, with the preserves and the Holy Rood Guild bringing in the majority of revenue to sustain the abbey. While life at Saint Joseph's was relatively self-sustaining, the brothers became interested in cementing a more viable future and began discussions about the feasibly of establishing a brewery in 2009.

The kettles at Spencer Brewery sit beside gargantuan windows facing the abbey's farmland. *Caroline Wallace*

CONVINCING THE COMMUNITIES

"Our size actually informed the decision [to start the brewery]. We still have some vitality," Father Isaac says. "You need that to pull it off and ultimately pay for it."

The idea of a brewery was very appealing to the monks. Apart from being a very interesting occupation to pick up in the abbey, overall brewing would be less labor intensive than the preserves. Where twelve to fourteen monks are needed to cook and package the jams, the brewhouse would call for only two. Even with the packaging of the beer, which remains the most intensive part of the process, the trade-off seemed clear that moving to brewing would free up more of the brothers to explore different roles at St. Joseph's.

With the community on board, a coalition of two brothers began the process of convincing the International Trappist Association of their preparedness for the undertaking. By proxy, all other Trappist breweries also got involved in the conversation.

After two years of touring the seven other Trappist breweries of the world at the time, where there was initially caution, hesitation,

and even a little apprehension about "what the Americans are going to do" to Trappist beer, the European parties eventually granted the Community at Spencer their blessing. . .with a few stipulations, like a state-of-the-art brewery, cellar, and packaging line.

"There are moments of a lot of interaction between communities, so it was important that everyone, especially the Belgian communities, be on board with us," Father Isaac says.

This intensive R&D cycle paid off in a really nice synthesis of all the knowledge of centuries of Trappist brewing practices. Construction broke ground in September 2012. On October 26, 2013, the first batch of Spencer Beer was brewed in the beautiful new brewery.

In the community a lot of changes had to take place to make way for the impending brewery. Part of the challenge for St. Joseph's Abbey was that many of the monks were not beer lovers to begin with, instead largely preferring wine. Cultivating a beer culture in the community has proven as important as creating a great set of recipes.

Spencer's branding story was developed by the community and Austin-based design firm Helms Workshop. *Caroline Wallace*

Initially, the four brothers involved with the brewery start-up process would take time out of their Friday afternoons to do tastings to educate their palates. They would open two craft beers a week, taste, and discuss. During this time they were also experimenting with recipes for their flagship beer on their pilot system in their old dairy barn as the brewery was being constructed. After five or six test batches, they were ready to expose the rest of the community to their process.

"We had to reach out to a wine-drinking crowd and give them something they would not only drink but enjoy," explains Father Isaac.

When all was said and drunk, they had created twenty-four pilot brews. While most were convinced they had nailed a recipe the community could be proud of, others weren't quite so sold.

"One monk to this day is convinced that pilot brew #18 was the beer we should be making," Father Isaac chuckles.

What they are making is a beer that does not conform perfectly to any style. During the beer's recipe conception there were a lot of expectations to make particular styles, but the brothers came to the realization that the first beer from any Trappist brewery must be a beer for the monks to drink, so they opted for a beer somewhat resembling a patersbier. Coming in at 6.5% and available in 11.2 oz (330 mL) and 750 mL bottles, Spencer Trappist Ale is a totally new take on Trappist beer.

To create a brand image fitting for the first American Trappist beer, the brothers recruited the talented designers at Helms Workshop in Austin, Texas. Before jumping in, the design team took time to understand who the brothers were.

"We collected everything we had published over the last fifty years and asked, 'What are the images we use the most to represent who we are?' The answer was the church tower," Father Isaac explains.

Armed with this knowledge, the design team set to work, returning twice as many iterations as the community originally contracted. What Helms Workshop's first choice turned out to be was the community's first choice as well: a simple image of the church's tower, blue and gold colors pulled from the coat of arms, the font used on the high altar inscription, and the words "Pair with Family and Friends."

Today the brothers' brewing team is made up of four brewing brothers, two admins to handle daily logistics, and an admin support team of three that meets monthly. For packaging needs there is an additional three or four younger brothers that step in to make packaging run smoothly. Additionally, there is always at least one laymen brew engineer on staff. Larry Littlehale, a brewer trained in Germany, currently serves as brewmaster.

The brothers are brewing one batch a week on their fifty barrel Krones system. Eventually, within the next five to ten years, the plan is to expand production about four times to 10,000 barrels annually. At that capacity the beer will be able to sustain the abbey alone. It is an arduous journey, getting familiar with creating so much output. It will take time for the brothers to get there, but space will not be an issue when they do.

"While planning the space with the ITA's recommendations in mind, we looked at our plans and said 'OK, let's do it and do it once,'" Father Isaac says.

BREWING AT SAINT JOSEPH'S

Below the grounds at St. Joseph's Abbey is an ancient glacial aquifer created by the melting of the Larentide Glacier over the last 18,000 years. It is from this underground aquifer that all of the water necessary for the production of beer is welled.

In terms of malt, the Trappist Ale calls for a combination of two and six row pils malts the brothers insist on sourcing from North American maltsters exclusively. There is a smaller collection of other malt varieties available to the brothers for their pilot batches, but because these pilot brews have yet to leave the abbey walls in a production capacity, they call for those in a much smaller amount.

The community is currently working with the University of Massachusetts Amherst developing an experimental barley program on a ten-acre plot on the monastery's property. They are also in the planning phases of experimenting with other grains that could be used in beer production. Eventually, the brothers would like to utilize these experimental grains they have grown on premises for pilot batches and small batch beer releases.

Other plans include partnering with a nearby brewer from Wormtown Brewery who is using locally sourced malt for his main production. Together they would want to establish a nearby source large enough to supplement both breweries' malt needs.

And what happens to the malt postmash? Spent grain goes to a local farmer the brothers work with. He uses the spent grain as feed for his cattle. He and other local farmers partner with the community to maintain and harvest the abbey's nearly 360 acres of hay annually.

Spencer's hop bill is made up of Willamette and Nugget hops sourced from Yakima valley. While the bitterness and aroma they contribute is important, the end goal for Spencer Trappist Ale is a balance of flavors, so the hop notes are subtle.

The brewhouse is a gleaming masterpiece. It faces the experimental barley fields and the early afternoon sun and sits in the gigantic windows that struck us upon our arrival.

In addition to being beautiful, the brewhouse is also incredibly effective. It is a semiautomated system that makes it impossible to skip a step in the process. The brothers make good use of their laboratory, though, checking the chemical and physical makeup of the beer several times during the brewing process.

The freshly brewed beer is clarified and piped into the 120-barrel fermentation tanks. Yeast is propagated on site and added to the tanks. There the wort and yeast will sit for around a week in active fermentation and a second week in maturation. At the end of the fermentation process, labs are taken to ensure the gravity, yeast vitality, and level of residual sugars remaining are all to spec for the beer. The beer is then clarified via centrifuge, rewarmed to kick-start the refermentation process, and piped into the on-site packaging facility.

Like most Trappist Ales, Spencer's flagship beer is fermented a second time in its glass bottle. This is problematic for an American Trappist brewery because American bottles lack the necessary thickness to withstand the second fermentation safely.

The fermenters at Spencer Brewery. *Caroline Wallace*

Bottling and packaging all take place at Spencer Brewery under the diligent eyes of the community and the brewery staff. *Caroline Wallace*

Bottles of Spencer Trappist Ale are packaged and distributed widely. *Caroline Wallace*

Inside the brewery bottles from every batch of Spencer Trappist Ale are archived for quality control and stored in the cellar.
Caroline Wallace

While there are thicker bottles being made privately for some American breweries, the brothers are forced to import bottles from Europe. There are an extra forty-two grams of glass in each bottle, making it a very expensive endeavor. This is a sustainable model in Europe, since breweries there will get multiple returns on a bottle, but the brothers at Spencer only get one, as America does not have the same recycling policies as Europe. The hope is to one day have a production capacity large enough to have a US-made bottle created, but that is a goal for the future.

The majority of the community's production is being packaged in 330 mL bottles sold in four-packs. This was their inaugural packaging choice. About a year later they expanded their shelf offering to include corked and caged 750 mL bottles of Trappist Ale and a small fleet of kegs.

The business plan long term is to skew more toward on-premise sales than off-premise. That has proven difficult initially because there is a flood of beers in the market and tap real estate is hard to pin down. It is important to the community to provide their beer to more people at an affordable price point.

"That's our niche in the market, so we'd better move on it," Father Isaac says.

Post-bottling, the beer is cellared for three weeks to allow time for the second bottle fermentation to occur. Then there is one more trip to the lab to check bottle pressure, IBUs, residual sugar levels, and taste before going to market.

To ensure quality once the beer has left the brewery's walls, the brothers hold back a few bottles of each batch in their immaculate backlit cellar. Each vintage is beautifully displayed should calls come in about issues with a particular batch.

While the Community at St. Joseph's strives to maintain a good relationship with the ITA and other Trappist breweries globally, there are many characteristics that set them apart from their European counterparts and suit an American market incredibly well.

The brothers are hugely experimental with their pilot system. They are brewing everything from strong Russian stouts, to traditional Belgian Quads, to Rye IPAs with Asian spices. It is a revolutionary idea that one day there could be an American Trappist Rye IPA on the market, but that sense of innovation and experimentation is prevalent in the evolving brew culture of America. It is logical to assume that these adventurous sensibilities exist within the walls of St. Joseph's Abbey as well.

Father Isaac and the community are defining three distinct lines in the Spencer Trappist Ale family: classics, seasonal releases, and limited releases.

Classics are the Belgian styles American beer drinkers expect from Trappist breweries but at domestic prices. Spencer's second foray into this space after their flagship beer is a strong, dark, high-bodied Belgian not unlike a Trappist Quadrupel style beer. The community released this in the winter of 2015 as a Trappist Holiday Ale. Separately, the brothers are considering what makes a great Trappist Tripel for future development.

Seasonal releases include familiar non-Belgian styles. There is an emerging trend of style loyalty in America that the community embraces and wants to support. Beers like robust stouts and East Coast IPAs would live in this category.

Finally, the limited release category will include beers that are, as the name implies, limited. With thoughts of spiced rye IPAs and barrel-aged Trappist Ale in the forefront of our minds, the sky's the limit for this category.

"The pilot system is fun. This is fun to do some product development and at the same time develop our own understanding of the American scene as we are evolving," Father Isaac explains.

To encourage development within the community, the brothers have established a beautiful brewing library. There is a long table covered in books, with chairs pulled out as if a group had only just stepped out after discussing their next pilot brew as Father Isaac shows us this room. The walls are adorned with happy photos of brew days and Abbey events. The library shelves are filled with books and resources, as well as one-off bottles of successful pilot brews and an

Spencer's library houses bottles of beer made on the brewery's pilot system, books on brewing and Trappist history, and a wide array of spices to supplement the community's and staff's education on all parts of the beer making process. *Caroline Wallace*

expansive sensory library consisting of spices and flavors often found in beers.

"One of the monks we are training in the brewery thought the library could benefit from a sensory resource so that when people say 'I smell cardamom' during a tasting, the rest of the group can smell cardamom," Father Isaac says.

It is such a simple idea, but so vital to the culture the monks at St. Joseph's Abbey are establishing. Beer is part of a dialogue.

We find in America alcohol consumption and beer consumption in general is stigmatized in a way not found in European culture. In places like Belgium, beer is revered. It is woven into the history. In America, often "beer" calls up images of red solo cups and drunk driving accidents. To combat that, Spencer pushes the importance of pairing higher alcohol beer with food and calls out how well Belgian beers pair with friends and family.

"Educating people is so immensely important," Father Isaac notes. He also explains to us that people in America are very much taken by the idea of monks brewing

beer right now. "I've run into it so often and with such strength that I feel there is something there with energy," he says. "Beer is such a connector. And one way or another, by monk or monastery, the divine is all very connected as well. As Christians we say 'built into human beings is some sort of desire for God.' There is an inherent desire for the absolute, an inner spiritual hunger. This beer is an easy connecter for folks who want a quiet, subtle link to the monastery and its spiritual values."

THE BEER

Spencer Trappist Ale (6.50% ABV)

Spencer Trappist Ale led the way for the brewery in 2013. Although it follows some style guidelines of a traditional patersbier, it is hotly debated what style classification it actually belongs in. And the brothers are just fine with that. It is a golden straw color, with a lovely lemony aroma and lots of yeast. It has a notable malt presence in the taste, with a nice hop balance coming in as you swallow and a very crisp finish. It is sold in 750 mL and 330 mL bottles. The smaller bottles are

A glass of Spencer Trappist Ale. *Caroline Wallace*

sold in four-packs, and both packaging choices are being distributed to an expanding circle of states.

Spencer Trappist Holiday Ale (8.70% ABV)

Spencer's sophomore release was rolled out in November 2015. It is a Belgian strong dark ale the brothers released under the moniker Trappist Holiday Ale. It pours a stately mahogany with red highlights and an off-white head. The nose smells of Belgian yeast, toasted biscuits, holiday spices, and dark, sweet caramel. The flavor is rich and sweet with notes of dark chocolate, brown bread, rum, spicy hops, holiday spices, honey, citrus, and burnt sugar. For being nearly 9.00% ABV, the alcohol is incredibly well hidden, making it a good contender for sharing at the holidays. It is available in 750 mL bottles throughout Massachusetts.

Spencer Trappist Imperial Stout (8.70% ABV)

Spencer's Trappist Imperial Stout was the brewery's first limited release, being marketed only for a short time in late winter 2015 through early spring 2016. Pouring an intense black color with lots of cocoa, coffee, and dark fruit on the nose and in the flavor, this riff on the Russian Imperial Stout is roasty, creamy, and decadent, with enough carbonation to remain silky. Coming in at 8.70% ABV, this limited release was packaged in 750 mL bottles.

Spencer Trappist IPA (7.20% ABV)

In 2016 Spencer released the first Trappist IPA to ever hit market shelves. A blend of Perle, Apollo, and Cascade hops gives this IPA its distinct hop character. Spencer touts that their IPA strikes a balance between the hop bill and the malt characteristics that differentiate it from other American IPAs. Coming in at 7.20% ABV, the Trappist IPA is available year-round in 12 oz bottles sold in a six-pack carrier.

Spencer Trappist Feierabendbier (4.70% ABV)

Pronounced fire-ah-bend-beer, this German libation's name translates to "the well-deserved beer." The style of the beer harkens back to the Trappist fundamental of manual labor and was brewed to be the perfect sip after a hard day's work. This Pilsner is straw colored with a light head. Nobel hops keep the flavor peppery and bitter with a crisp finish. The Trappist Feierabendbier is available in 12 oz bottles sold in a six-pack carrier.

Spencer Trappist Festive Lager (7.50% ABV)

Released in fall 2016 as a seasonal, Spencer's Trappist Festive Lager is a traditional German autumnal lager made with a balance of Vienna and smoked malts. Nobel hops add a spicy undertone and a bitter finish to the caramel, almost treacle-like flavor. At 7.50% ABV the alcohol content is high for the style, but the monks call out cheekily that is why they call it festive. The russet suds are available seasonally in the fall in 12 oz bottles sold in a six-pack carrier.

TRAVEL TIPS

While the abbey does not permit tours of the brewery or the jam factory, there is a gift shop off the main road that sells jams and jellies, beer glasses, and craft items produced by the monks. Visitors are permitted to join in mass services and walk the well-manicured paths.

Though visiting opportunities are short, St. Joseph's Abbey is only sixty miles from Boston, Massachusetts, an incredibly bustling urban area with a plethora of attractions for beer drinkers and non–beer drinkers alike.

The abbey shop at St. Joseph's Abbey. *Caroline Wallace*

13. Contemplation

Craft beer is experiencing tremendous growth, especially in American markets. In 2015 craft beer sales increased 17.6%, while demand for imported beers increased by nearly 7%. When all has been said and the bottles are empty, craft beer is a $20 billion market.

The number of Trappist abbeys interested in brewing and selling their ales has also increased in recent time. In just five years Saint Joseph's Abbey, Abdij Maria Toevlucht, Engelszell Abbey, and Abbazia delle Tre Fontane have all gone through the rigors of obtaining ITA label approval to produce and market their beers. As recently as March 2016, Monasterio de San Pedro de Cardena, a current ITA member in Northern Spain, began developing and brewing its own beer recipe, the Cardena Tripel. Although the process can take years, the Monasterio appears to be in the early steps of applying for label approval to certify the Cardena Tripel as an Authentic Trappist Product. While the monastery at San Pedro de Cardena has stood for over one thousand years, in as little as two years it could become the twelfth monastery to join the ranks of Chimay, Rochefort, and Westmalle.

Even with the calculated growth we have seen in the number of Trappist breweries, the monks are not in the brewing game to capitalize on that $20 billion craft beer pot. Still, their beers stand out as exceptional among craft beer drinkers. Many of the beers are ranked among the best in the world, and few boast less than an outstanding rating on sites like RateBeer.com, BeerAdvocate.com, and Untappd.

The demand on such a small reserve of Trappist beer has resulted in some unsavory consequences. Westvleteren 12 can only be purchased either at the abbey's gates or at the In de Vrede Café nearby, but is then sometimes resold at incredible markups to the end consumer. Likewise, Spencer Trappist Ales are

Thousands of bottles are sanitized and refilled with Trappist beers each day. *Jessica Deahl*

priced slightly higher than the monks of Saint Joseph's Abbey would advise. They would like to lower the prices closer to those of domestic beers, but negotiating those desires with a growing population of beer drinkers thirsty for Trappist Ales can be tricky.

It is of little surprise that the industry finds itself in such a state. There is a national push toward artisan, thoughtful foods and beverages. Heirloom cocktails, regional seed collecting, and a resurgence of antiquated techniques in food and beverage preparation are all prevalent in American culinary circles. Add to this the inherent standard of exceptional quality Trappist beers are held to by the International Trappist Association; the careful sourcing of hops and malt; the historical recipes and brewing processes; and the consistently well-balanced, flavorful end products, and there is little room left for guessing what makes Trappist beer the heavily sought after commodity it is on American craft beer shelves.

American brewers are taking pages out of the books of Belgian beer makers to bring a taste of that exceptionally high quality beer to local taprooms across the nation. Many well-established American breweries are emulating the monastic tradition of brewing through the production of abbey-style ales, attracting new, curious beer drinkers to these American reinterpretations of centuries-old beers. These American reinterpretations of Abbey ales and Belgian styles act as many American beer drinkers' first foray into craft beer. Often American Belgo-style ales drive American markets directly to the doors of Westvleteren and Tre Fontane for a revered sip of true Trappist beers.

Still, the importance of respecting the Trappist name cannot be understated. In its many years of advocacy work for the Trappist communities, one of the International Trappist Association's highest priorities has been to defend the Authentic Trappist Product trademark (as well as the distinction of excellent quality that trademark implies) against breweries seeking to use the name Trappist in their non-Trappist wares.

While the global outcry for more Trappist beer may be loud, it fails to sway the production goals of many of the Trappist communities we have discussed. Monks brew to live; they do not live to brew. It is a mechanism for sustaining their way of life, and it is that disregard for economic growth and renown that makes Trappist beers so enigmatic to beer drinkers.

Americans are indoctrinated early on to images of happy, red-faced monks drinking oversized goblets of dark Abbey ale throughout beer marketing, but when Trappist culture is brought up, for the most part people think only of somber, silent monks brewing a beer that they almost resent for the attention it brings on the community.

The truth lies somewhere in between the happy monk and the austere brewer, as we hope you have discovered during our tour. The Trappist monks we have encountered take their wares and way of life very seriously. They've devoted themselves to a very challenging lifestyle and do have some of the assumed sober rituals and traditions that seem to isolate them from the world.

But Trappist monks are also quietly proud of their beer and are excited to know that three American women would travel halfway across the world to learn about it. They are intrigued that outside of the walls to which they have been devoted, there is a whole world having experiences and making memories with their beers in hand.

Individually, they have eyes that dance when they tell jokes, and they are not men unwilling to correct very directly the idyllic pictures we, as Americans, sometimes paint of them.

Trappist monks are quiet men, to be sure, but are not out of touch. They can see the world they have turned away from and appreciate its curiosity of their way of life. They do not have disdain or resentment toward their beers. In fact, they often see them as their conduit to the world outside. They are a tiny witness to us of the brothers' way of life and a small token of hope that we may glean a sliver of their deep connection to the absolute.

The Abbot of Engelszell flashes the photographer a thumbs-up. *Caroline Wallace*

Thanks to Our Interpreters

Without the help of these incredible men and women—Filip "Phil" Muylle, Océane Crabbe, Linda Mous, Bart Westerveld, and Alina Brückner—we would never had made it past "hello" at many of our interviews, so to you, our friends, we say merci, dank u, danke, and thank you!

FROM LEFT TO RIGHT: Océane Crabbe. Filip "Phil" Muylle. Linda Mous. Bart Westerveld. Alina Brückner. *Caroline Wallace*

References

"The Abbey." Tre Fontane. 2015. Accessed November 24, 2015. http://www.abbaziatrefontane.it/.

"Abdij Van de Trappisten Van Westmalle." Abdij Van de Trappisten Van Westmalle. Accessed June 13, 2015. http://www.trappistwestmalle.be/.

"Achel | Shelton Brothers." Shelton Brothers. Accessed November 10, 2015. http://www.sheltonbrothers.com/breweries/achel/.

"Achelse Kluis." Achelse Kluis. Accessed November 10, 2015. http://www.achelsekluis.org/pageNL/home.html.

"America's First Trappist Beer." Spencer Trappist Ale. Accessed November 10, 2015. http://spencerbrewery.com/beer/.

Attwater, Donald, and Catherine Rachel John. *The Penguin Dictionary of Saints*. 3rd ed. London: Penguin Books, 1995.

"Augustinus De Lestrange Dubosc." *World Heritage Encyclopedia*. Accessed June 13, 2015. http://www.gutenberg.us/articles/augustinus_de_lestrange_dubosc.

Bertoniere, Gabriel. *Through Faith & Fire: The Monks of Spencer, 1825–1958*. New York: Yorkville Press, 2005.

"Bières De Chimay." Accessed November 28, 2015. http://belgium.beertourism.com/belgian-breweries/bieres-de-chimay.

Bland, Alastair. "If You're Toasting to Health, Reach for Beer, Not (Sparkling) Wine." NPR. 2015. Accessed November 29, 2015. http://www.npr.org/sections/thesalt/2014/12/31/374187472/if-youre-toasting-for-health-beer-may-be-a-good-bet.

Bordon, Fabrice. "Chimay." Interview by authors. June 11, 2015.

"The Brewery in the History of Orval." Orval Abbey. 2011. Accessed September 30, 2015. http://www.orval.be/en/.

Brother Benedikt. "Westmalle." Interview by authors. June 15, 2015.

Brother Christiaan. "Zundert." Interview by authors. June 16, 2015.

Brother Godfried. "Westvleteren." Interview by authors. June 13, 2015.

Brother Guido. "Zundert." Interview by authors. June 16, 2015.

Brother Isaac. "La Trappe." Interview by authors. June 9, 2015.

Brother Joris. "Westvleteren." Interview by authors. June 13, 2015.

"Brouwerij Der Sint-Benedictusabdij De Achelse Kluis." Brouwerij Der Sint-Benedictusabdij De Achelse Kluis. Accessed November 10, 2015. http://belgium.beertourism.com/belgian-breweries/de-achelse-kluis.

"Brouwerij Westmalle." Brouwerij Westmalle. Accessed June 13, 2015. http://belgium.beertourism.com/belgian-breweries/brouwerij-westmalle.

"Chimay: A True Belgian Beer." *Hops Magazine*. July 4, 2011. Accessed November 28, 2015. http://www.hopsmagazine.com/chimay-a-true-belgian-beer/.

"The Chimay Trappist Beers, Official Video in English." March 23, 2011. Accessed November 28, 2015. https://www.youtube.com/watch?v=sTbTzINcj1w.

Clay, James. "Abbey Notre-Dame De Scourmont." Accessed November 28, 2015. http://www.jamesclay.co.uk/core/brewery-story/chimay/abbey-notre-dame-de-scourmont.

"The Complex." Tre Fontane. 2015. Accessed November 24, 2015. http://www.abbaziatrefontane.it/.

Daniele, Sergio. "Tre Fontane." Interview by authors. June 18, 2015.

"Domus Leuven." Domus Leuven. Accessed November 10, 2015. http://www.domusleuven.be/p_brouwerij_en.html.

Dzen, Gary. "Year-Old Trappist Brewery in Spencer Expands Its Line." BostonGlobe.com. September 28, 2015. Accessed December 10, 2015. https://www.bostonglobe.com/lifestyle/food-dining/2015/09/28/year-old-trappist-brewery-spencer-expands-its-line/r2vRU9BSjhbnzmUnzcHPSI/story.html.

Father Isaac. "Spencer." Interview by authors. June 22, 2015.

"Foundation and Expansion." Abbaye Notre-Dame De Citeaux. Accessed August 23, 2015. http://www.citeaux-abbaye.com/en/the-cistercians-yesterday-today-tomorrow/premier-article-anglais/fondation-and-expansion.

Fourneau, A. *L'abbaye Notre-Dame de Saint-Remy à Rochefort: Histoire d'une communauté cistercienne en terre de Famenne.* Abbaye Notre-Dame de Saint-Remy. Rochefort, 2002

Frisque, Xavier. "Orval Brewery and ITA." Interview by authors. June 5, 2015.

Harding, Stephen. "Carta Caritatis Posterior: The Charter of Charity." Cistercian.org. Accessed August 23, 2015. https://www.cistercian.org/abbey/our-life/pdf/Carta Caritatis Posterior.pdf.

Hauseder, Abbot Marianus. "Stift Engelszell." Interview by authors. June 17, 2015.

Henroz, Philippe. "Orval Brewery." Interview by authors. June 5, 2015.

Hieronymus, Stan. *Brew Like a Monk: Trappist, Abbey, and Strong Belgian Ales and How to Brew Them.* Boulder, CO: Brewers Publications, 2005.

History of Christianity. Lecture 20 of 30. The Cluniac & Cistercian Revivals. Stylus Productions, 2013. Film.

"Home—Chimay." Chimay. Accessed November 28, 2015. http://chimay.com/us/.

"How Orval Beer Is Made." Orval Abbey. 2011. Accessed September 30, 2015. http://www.orval.be/en/.

"International Trappist Association: Westvleteren." International Trappist Association. Accessed November 1, 2015. http://www.trappist.be/en/pages/monasteries-westvleteren.

International Trappist Association, *Products: Trappist Beers*

International Trappist Association, *Who We Are*, 2010

"Interview with Westvleteren's Brother Joris." In *High and Mighty Beer Show.* Dan Shelton. December 15, 2012.

Jackson, Michael. "Michael Jackson's Beer Hunter—Visiting the Brand-New Trappist Brewery." Accessed November 10, 2015. http://beerhunter.com/documents/19133-001464.html.

"Jean-Armand Le Bouthillier De Rance." Original Catholic Encyclopedia. Accessed June 13, 2015. http://oce.catholic.com/index.php?title=Jean-Armand_Le_Bouthillier_de_Rance.

Jungwirth, Jennifer. "Stift Engelszell." Interview by authors. June 17, 2015.

Knops, Marc. "Achel." Interview by authors. June 8, 2015.

"Location Zundert, Vincent Van GoghHuis—Van Gogh Brabant." Accessed November 12, 2015. http://www.vangoghbrabant.com/en/locaties/zundert.

"A Long History." Orval Abbey. 2011. Accessed September 30, 2015. http://www.orval.be/en/.

"Malle." Accessed June 13, 2015. https://en.wikipedia.org/wiki/Malle#16th_to_18th_century.

Matarasso, Pauline, ed. *The Cistercian World: Monastic Writings of the Twelfth Century.* New York: Penguin, 2006.

Minet, Benoît. "Rochefort." Interview by authors. June 10, 2015.

Montanari, Sergio Peer. *L'Abbazia Delle Tre Fontane.* Edited by Alessandro Maria Barelli. Translated by Virginia Grego. Rome: Historia Associazione Culturale, 1967.

New World Encyclopedia contributors. "Cistercians." New World Encyclopedia. Accessed August 8, 2015. http://www.newworldencyclMopedia.org/p/index.php?title=Cistercians&oldid=969419.

"A Newcomer's Guide to the Trappists." Trappists.org. Accessed September 5, 2015. http://www.trappists.org/newcomers

Obrecht, E. (1911). "Notre-Dame de Molesme." In *The Catholic Encyclopedia.* New York: Robert Appleton Company, 1911. Retrieved August 2, 2015, from New Advent: http://www.newadvent.org/cathen/10433b.htm.

"Observantiae: Continuity and Reforms in the Cistercian Family." International Association of Lay Cistercian Communities. September 14, 2002. Accessed July 15, 2015. http://www.cistercianfamily.org/documents/Observantiae english.pdf.

"Our History." Spencer Abbey. Accessed November 15, 2015. http://www.spencerabbey.org/our-history/.

"Our History: Cistercian Beginnings." Saint Joseph's Abbey. Accessed August 8, 2015. http://www.spencerabbey.org/our-history/cistercian-beginnings/.

"Our Story." La Trappe. Accessed November 22, 2015. http://www.latrappetrappist.com/en/.

Pennington, Basil. "The Cistercians: An Introductory History by M. Basil Pennington, OCSO." The Order of Saint Benedict. 2005. Accessed October 24, 2015. http://www.osb.org/cist/intro.html.

"Protecting the Trappist Name." International Trappist Association. Accessed November 29, 2015. http://www.trappist.be/en/pages/protected-trademark.

Protz, Roger. "Achel Trappist Brewery, Belgium." Accessed November 10, 2015. http://www.beer-pages.com/stories/achel.htm.

Rail, Evan. "Something Is Brewing in Austria Far from Flanders: Engelszell Abbey Is Making a Trappist Beer in the Style of the Low Countries." *Wall Street Journal,* September 6, 2012 (Food & Drink section). Accessed November 5, 2015. http://www.wsj.com/articles/SB10000872396390443618604577623402391203464.

"Region of Abbey Maria Toevlucht, Zundert." Accessed November 12, 2015. http://www.tastesofabbeys.com/abbeys/region-of-abbey-maria-toevlucht-zundert.

"Region of Notre-Dame De Scourmont Abbey, Chimay." Accessed November 28, 2015. http://www.tastesofabbeys.com/abbeys/region-of-notre-dame-de-scourmont-abbey-chimay.

"Resurrection." Orval Abbey. 2011. Accessed September 30, 2015. http://www.orval.be/en/.

"Rochefort 6." BeerTourism.com. 2015. Accessed July 20, 2015. http://belgium.beertourism.com/belgian-beers/rochefort-6.

"Rochefort 8." BeerTourism.com. 2015. Accessed July 20, 2015. http://belgium.beertourism.com/belgian-beers/rochefort-8.

"Rochefort 10." BeerTourism.com. 2015. Accessed July 20, 2015. http://belgium.beertourism.com/belgian-beers/rochefort-10.

"Saint Joseph's Abbey 1950–Present." Accessed November 15, 2015. http://www.spencerabbey.org/our-history/saint-josephs-abbey-1950-2015/.

Sapens, Paul. *Bier in Alle Eeuwidgheid: 125 Jaar Trappistenbrouwerij De Koningshoeven 1884–2009*. Uitgeverij Pix4Profs, 2009.

Sites Cisterciens D'Europe (Cistercian Sites in Europe). *Antwerpen: Charte Européenne Des Abbayes Et Sites Cistercians*, 2013.

"Spiritual Heights and Depths." Orval Abbey. 2011. Accessed September 30, 2015. http://www.orval.be/en/.

"Stift Engelszell." Accessed November 4, 2015. http://www.stift-engelszell.at/.

"Stift Engelszell Trappistenbier." Pamphlet, Engelhartszell. Stift Engelszell

"Taste the Silence." La Trappe. Accessed October 28, 2015. http://www.latrappetrappist.com/en/.

Theisen, Jerome. "OSB. About the Rule of Saint Benedict by Abbot Primate Jerome Theisen OSB." May 18, 2015. Accessed August 2, 2015.

Theuwen, Jordy. "Achel." Interview by authors. June 8, 2015.

"Train Explosion Hamont." Accessed November 10, 2015. http://www.grevenbroekmuseum.be/index.php/en/world-war-i-1914-1918/train-explosion-hamont.

"Trappist Achel—Belgian Beer Specialist." October 9, 2013. Accessed November 10, 2015. http://drinkbelgianbeer.com/breweries/trappist-achel.

"Trappist Ales." La Trappe. Accessed October 28, 2015. http://www.latrappetrappist.com/en/.

"Trappist Beers: Rochefort." International Trappist Association. Accessed August 15, 2015. http://www.trappist.be/en/pages/trappist-beers-rochefort.html.

"Useful Information." Tre Fontane. 2015. Accessed December 5, 2015. http://www.abbaziatrefontane.it/.

Van Assche, Philippe. "Westmalle." Interview by authors. June 15, 2015.

"Visit us." La Trappe. Accessed December 1, 2015. http://www.latrappetrappist.com/en/.

Watson, Bart. "National Beer Sales & Production Data—Brewers Association." Brewers Association. Accessed November 30, 2015. https://www.brewersassociation.org/statistics/national-beer-sales-production-data/.

"Who We Are." OCSO: Order of Cistercians of the Strict Observance. 2010. Accessed August 18, 2015. http://www.ocso.org/who-we-are/our-identity.

Glossary

Abbey: A monastery under the supervision of an abbot.

Abbey beers: A catch-all term for beers brewed by non-Trappist monastic orders or commercial breweries mimicking the Belgian styles typically associated with monastic brewing. Not to be confused with Trappist beers.

Abbot: An ecclesiastical title given to the head, or father, of an abbey.

Ale: A style of beer made with top fermenting yeast.

Arable: Suitable or used for agriculture.

Authentic Trappist Product: Guarantees the monastic origin of the products and ensures the quality and traditional standards rooted in the monastic life of a Trappist community.

Barrel (bbl): A measure of liquid used commonly in beer; 1 bbl is equal to thirty-one gallons.

Benedictine: A monastic order founded to follow the Rule of Saint Benedict.

Bottle fermentation: A form of fermentation that typically follows traditional fermentation methods. In bottle fermentation, a small addition of yeast and sugar is added to beer as it is injected into the bottle. This creates carbonation in the beer and allows the beer to continue developing in flavor and complexity as it ages.

Coadjutor bishop: A bishop designated to help the diocesan bishop in the administration of the diocese.

Community: A group of monastics established and bound by a place or specific purpose.

Diocese: A district under the care of a bishop.

Dry hop: An additional round of hopping that takes place during fermentation. The practice of dry hopping began centuries ago in Britain, when brewers discovered that adding extra hops to a cask of beer just before it was shipped off to the customer would give it an extra dose of hop flavor and aroma.

Fermenter: A vessel that maintains optimal conditions for the growth of microorganisms used in large-scale fermentation. In other words, where beer becomes beer.

Fromager: Someone who makes cheese.

Guesthouse: Living quarters reserved for guests on spiritual retreats at monasteries

Hectoliter (hL): The metric measure for beer production; 1 hL is equal to 26.5 gallons

Kettle: An important component of the brewing process; the kettle is the vessel in which the wort is brought to a boil and additions of hops are added for aroma and flavor.

International Trappist Association: A nonprofit association composed of monasteries of the Cistercian Order of the Strict Observance formed to protect the "Trappist" trademark and protect their common interests.

Lager: A type of beer that is produced at low temperatures using bottom-fermenting yeast.

Layperson: An unordained person.

Monastery: A building or buildings occupied by a community of monks or nuns living under religious vows.

Novice: A member of the religious community that has taken the first steps to becoming a brother or sister of a given order.

Priory: A monastery under the supervision of a prior.

Refectory: The room dedicated to meals in a monastery.

The Rule of Saint Benedict: Precepts written by Saint Benedict of Nursia (c. 480–547) for monks living under the authority of an abbot.

Savigniac Order: A monastic order founded at the abbey of Savigny in northern France.

Spent grain: A by-product of the brewing process. When malt is boiled, the starches are converted to sugars. The remaining husks of the malt are referred to as spent grain.

Trappist: A monk in the Order of Cistercians of the Strict Observance, a religious order of the Roman Catholic Church.

Trappistine: A nun in the Order of Cistercians of the Strict Observance, a religious order of the Roman Catholic Church.

Trappist pubs: Pubs that were contracted to serve Trappist produced beers exclusively during the mid-1900s.

Yeast: A microscopic organism that plays a crucial role in beer making. Yeast is injected into wort or beer to consume sugars and produce alcohol and carbonation.